RENEGADE TEA COOKBOOK

VOICES OF THE DEAD SERIES: COMPANION

BY JO WILEY, AS TOLD TO VICTORIA RASCHKE
ILLUSTRATED BY MADELINE ROSE

ALSO BY VICTORIA RASCHKE

Who by Water - Voices of the Dead: Book One

Our Lady of the Various Sorrows -
Voices of the Dead: Book Two

Like a Pale Moon - Voices of the Dead: Book Three

Strange As Angels - Voices of the Dead: Book Four

ACKNOWLEDGMENTS

This cookbook exists because people who visited Renegade Tea in the Voices of the Dead books wanted to enjoy Jo's brownies or one of Fred's soups. Therefore, the first thank you goes to everyone who asked for a recipe. I secretly always wanted to write a cookbook, and now I've had the pleasure of doing so.

An enormous thank you goes out to everyone who helped test recipes. I was thrilled that anyone agreed to do it and even more impressed with their dedication to finding ingredients and sending me feedback in the middle of a pandemic. Their time, efforts, and thoughtful notes on the recipes have made them better and, I hope, easier for you to follow at home. If you make something and love it, know that Mia Wilson, Jeanne Griswold, John Mott, Shelley Kubitz Mahannah, Annie Peterle, Laura Zumwalt, Janey Stevens, Heather Smith, and Amy Morrison all had a hand in it. A special thank you goes to Julian Raschke and Su Fertall, my son and his partner. They took on a huge number of recipes despite their work schedules, the pandemic, and a concussion (he's fully recovered). I can't wait for you two to get that cat cafe-bookstore-bakery open so I can have a cup of tea and one of your potice in person. Thank you also to Karl Sigler, who shared his go-to recipe for pain de mie and is an inspirational home baker in his own right.

Jennifer Goode Stevens was on board again as my editor. She is a force for clarity in writing and helps me fight my overly poetic angels and my spelling demons. The multi-talented and remarkable Madeline Rose joined our team this time as the illustrator; she did the magical drawings throughout. She also happens to be my niece, which means I get to brag. keifel agostini, my partner in the adventures of life in general and publishing in particular, designed the cover and interior and handled all of the processes required to get this book into your hands or onto your e-reader. He is also a typography nerd, hence his preference for not capitalizing his name.

Finally, I wouldn't have ever been interested in cooking and baking if not for the people in my life who loved to cook and shared their knowledge and recipes. My parents, Doris and Bill Raschke, were both wonderful cooks, and I feel their presence in my own kitchen when I make their recipes. You will get a taste of their combined efforts if you make Jo's Chili and Cornbread. My grandmother Evelyn and my aunts and great aunts on both sides—Louise, Evelyn, Peggy, Edith Mary, Daisy, Thelma, and Nancy—all contributed to the cook I am with their recipes and patience. And though I never got to meet her, my grandmother Edith Victoria's Swedish meatball recipe is my go-to. This doesn't even get to the recipes shared among friends, cousins, siblings, and my children, because that list would make this acknowledgment longer than the book. I also had the good fortune to go to culinary school in what now seems like a different life. Chef Tom Loftis and Dr. Ken Morlino both ran a tight ship and made me a better, more disciplined, and more curious cook. I hope they aren't too disappointed I'm not cooking for a living anymore.

For absent friends

CONTENTS

SPELLS & STUFF

INDEX

INTRODUCTION

Renegade Teahouse started as three friends dreaming over beers. Vesna and I wanted to stop working for other people, and Gregor wanted to go to a teahouse that served decent food as well as warm drinks. Vesna and I convinced him to go with the punk teahouse theme because none of us were British or into that cozy grandma vibe. We also weren't going to be serving the high-end desserts that can be found in the grand old coffeehouses of Eastern Europe. Neither Vesna nor I had those kind of baking skills, and we were only going to offer tea and a scone or two in the beginning.

As if by magic, Gregor had a spot open up in the building his family owned on Zajčeva ulica in Staro mesto. We scraped together the required permits, enough battered furniture, a stack of gig posters, the necessary equipment and wares, and threw open our doors. I would love to say we were immediately embraced by all of Ljubljana and that young, old, and in-between made their way to us daily for their fix of caffeine and the Ramones. But that is, of course, not how it happened. We were open for three days when the bathroom downstairs flooded. Initially customers who were looking for an afternoon tea and Vivaldi vibe were turned off by the loud music and mismatched everything. And the younger crowd who loved the music and the vibe weren't sure what to make of a tower of scones and dainty tea sandwiches. We also couldn't keep a dishwasher for longer than two months.

Then Fred found us, and the food menu got rounded out with soups and some other daily specials. We added a stash of off-menu coffee for the tea-haters. Tea kind of had a cultural moment again. Ten years in, we hired Maja—who was a better baker than Vesna, Fred, and I combined—and everything gelled. We'd been written about on tourist sites, won some awards for our food, and built a community around our open mic nights and the bands who played regularly. (Shout out to Mia and Liar's Knot for being with us from the beginning.)

As we were starting to look at evolving into our next phase, the world turned sideways and kind of caught on fire. I won't go into it here, but come by sometime and I'll give you the short version. The teahouse eventually staggered and swayed into its next iteration, and we're still here—if you know how to find us. We still serve the very best soups made with love and attention by Fred, who is now an owner along with Reka, our one long-haul dishwasher. Ivanka has taken over much of the baking, though I keep my hand in when I'm not helping Gregor run the inn we also manage now. Our community might be a little smaller—and a lot weirder—than it was, but it's tighter and more important to us than ever.

By popular request, I put this book together with a lot of help from Vesna, Fred, and Ivanka. It covers much of what we are known for at the teahouse, some things we like to make at home, and a few non-culinary thoughts about being witchy in the world. I'm glad a copy has fallen into your hands, however that may have occurred. If you already knew about Renegade Tea, I hope it will tide you over until you can find your way back. If this is your introduction to us, welcome.

A FEW QUICK THOUGHTS ON TEA

Though I run a teahouse, I would never proclaim myself a tea expert. People study and work for years to earn the title of tea sommelier. I am, however, a lover of tea and like to treat it well. We choose our teas to go with the menu at the teahouse, and we offer a range of caffeine-free to full-test teas. If you ask nicely and Fred is in the mood, he will also make you an off-menu Turkish coffee, but don't go bragging to all your friends about it. Quantities of coffee and Fred's patience are limited.

It you want to learn more about tea, you can find a plethora of books on the history, culture, and proper preparation of this most wondrous plant. There is undoubtedly a whole section on it at your local library. I recommend *The Tea Enthusiast's Handbook* and *The Story of Tea* by Mary Lou Heiss as jumping off points. If you really want to get into tea, I feel it's important to learn about the dark side of tea history. Its cultivation and sale fueled empires and colonization. In some places in the world, the production of tea still exploits labor and the environment, so it's important to know where your tea comes from, as well as who grows it, how they are treated, and how well the land is cared for.

There is a lot to know and learn, but the basics of getting a good cup are simple. I've included information on caffeine levels, as many come to tea for a kindler, gentler approach to their drug of choice or to avoid caffeine altogether. Let me be clear, all tea made from *Camellia sinensis* has caffeine unless it has been decaffeinated. Even then it will have some residual caffeine. Herbal teas, more accurately tisanes or decoctions, are made from all kinds of plant matter, fresh and dried, that is not tea. Some of these do contain caffeine and other stimulants but are, for the most part, caffeine-free.

CAFFEINE

Teas ranked least to most caffeinated with some signposts to help judge.

Herbal tisanes or decoctions - caffeine free*
Rooibos or red tea - caffeine free
Decaf teas - still contain trace amounts of caffeine
Hot cocoa or chocolate
White tea
Green tea
Oolong tea
Black tea
Matcha
Yerba maté
Coffee

*Unless blended with kava, yerba maté, kola, cocoa beans, guarana, or other herbal caffeine sources. Always check labels or ask.

BREW TIMES AND TEMPERATURES

These are my best suggestions, but you may find brewing at lower temperatures or for longer or shorter times suits you better. There will be a difference in results depending on whether you are using tea bags or loose tea. For herbal tisanes or decoctions, the times and temperatures vary so widely—from one to two minutes in boiling water to overnight in the fridge—a good herbal handbook would be a wise investment if you want to get into these "non-tea" teas. I've offered a ballpark for your average commercial herbal tea blend. Matcha is a whole other process, which I have not included as we don't offer it at the shop. Again there is a wealth of information out there to get you headed in the right direction.

Herbal tisanes - 210°F/100°C for 3-6 minutes

Rooibos or red tea - 210°F/100°C for 5-10 minutes

White tea - 155°F/70°C for 1-2 minutes

Green tea - 175°F/80°C for 1-2 minutes

Oolong tea - 185°F/85°C for 2-3 minutes

Black tea - 210°F/100°C for 2-3 minutes

NOTES ON THE RECIPES

These recipes are designed for home cooks working in home kitchens. Where specialty equipment or hard to find ingredients are called for, substitutions for techniques and ingredients have been offered. All of the recipes were tested in home kitchens using U.S. volumetric measurements. Metric weight conversions have been included for convenience, but recipes were not retested using these measurements.

Different kinds of salt have different levels of saltiness. I've tried to specify the kind of salt that should be used in each recipe, but please salt cooked dishes to your taste. In baking recipes, the amount of salt required is more precise in order to achieve the best results.

Ingredients are mostly referred to using U.S. terms.

All eggs are U.S. grade large (~2 ounces or 57g), except where noted.

Baking ingredients should be at room temperature before starting the recipe.

Please follow your country's guidelines for home canning or preserving.

RENEGADE TEA SPECIALS

We offer a full tea service at Renegade Tea, as well as an à la carte menu. The three-tiered curate stand holds three plates and food enough for one to two people. Traditionally, the top tier will include scones or seasonal breads. The second tier consists of sandwiches and savories, and the bottom tier is for sweets.

The accepted etiquette suggests the courses be eaten in the order of sandwiches and savories, followed by scones and seasonal breads, and ending with sweets. A fourth course of cake or trifle or seasonal fruit that is served separately can be added. All courses are served with tea, but the sweets and cake course can be served with champagne or sherry. We don't serve alcohol at Renegade Tea except for private parties. Etiquette be damned, I say eat the scones while they are warm and then dig into the rest of it. No one here will whack the back of your hand with the Big Book of Stuffy Nonsense, so you do you. I do suggest ordering soup for whichever course you choose. It's what we are known for, and I wouldn't want you to miss out.

Producing a multi-course, multi-option tea is more work than most of us would want to tackle at home. A sandwich and a sweet, or a soup and sandwich combo with a sweet is more doable and won't have you in the kitchen all day if you don't want to be.

RECIPES FOR THE TOP PLATE OF THE TEA SERVICE

RENEGADE TEA SCONE BASIC RECIPE

Makes 12

At the teahouse we make huge batches of scones, but this recipe is pared down for a home kitchen. They come together fast and don't bake long, so they can be thrown together in the morning while you're making coffee, or tea. For the record, our take on scones is closer to what you would find in an American coffeehouse than in a British tea shop. It may be sacrilegious to say so, but I prefer these.

3 1/2 cups (15.75 ounces/500g) all-purpose flour

2 tablespoons sugar

2 teaspoons baking powder

1 teaspoon baking soda

1 teaspoon coarse kosher salt or 1/2 teaspoon fine sea salt

1/3 cup (60g) dried Zante currants (I like my scones heavy on the fruit and usually bump this up to a 1/2 cup.)

1 cup (240mL) buttermilk

1 large egg

8 tablespoons (1 stick/4 ounces/114g) unsalted butter

2 tablespoons coarse natural sugar (turbinado, Sugar in the Raw)

Preheat oven to 400°F (205°C).

In a large bowl, whisk together flour, sugar, baking powder, baking soda, and salt. Stir currants into the dry mixture to coat them with flour; this will help them stay more evenly distributed in the final mixture and in the scones. Melt butter on stove top or in the microwave and let cool slightly. In a separate bowl, whisk together buttermilk and egg, then drizzle in melted butter slowly while whisking.

Pour wet mixture over dry (save whatever remains in the wet mixture bowl to glaze the tops with) and stir together with a fork, just until the dry ingredients are incorporated. You may have to add a splash more of the buttermilk depending on how dry your flour is or how humid the day is or whatever phase the moon is in. The mixture will be tattered and shaggy looking, like a biscuit (American, not British) dough.

Dump the dough out onto a lightly floured counter or board and gently press the dough together. I would say knead, but really you want to turn it no more than three or four times. Shape together into a fat log and divide into three equal portions with your kitchen witch knife or a bench scraper. Shape each portion into a thick disc about 4 inches (10cm) across and cut into four equal pieces through the center—like cutting a pie into four. Place scones on a lined (parchment or reusable baking mat) baking sheet, one row pointed one direction and the new row pointed the opposite direction, with at least 1 1/2 inches (3-4cm) between. Using a pastry brush, glaze the top of each scone with whatever is left of the wet mixture in the bowl. if you don't have enough you can pour in a splash more of buttermilk, or plain milk if you've used all your buttermilk in the recipe. Sprinkle the tops with a little bit of the coarse natural sugar. You can use regular granulated sugar if you don't have the coarse kind, or you can skip the sugar altogether.

Bake for 20-25 minutes or until the tops are just golden brown and the bottoms are browned. You can also tap the bottoms to see if they sound a little bit hollow. It doesn't work as well as it does with bread, but once you make them a few times you'll know the right sound. Serve hot with jam and butter or clotted cream. They're also good at room temperature, but they are best eaten the same day.

Notes: You can substitute plain yogurt or sour cream for the buttermilk. The texture will be a little different, but it works. You may have to add a splash of regular milk if the mixture is too dry. You can substitute up to about half of the flour with whole wheat or other whole grain flour for a denser, heartier scone.

To make a vegan version of the recipe, you can substitute the buttermilk with a nondairy milk or yogurt and the butter for coconut oil or a light-tasting vegetable oil. You can leave out the egg altogether, but the scones will have a slightly drier, more biscuit-like texture and you may need to add more of the nondairy substitute you are using to get the dough to come together.

Variations on a theme:

You can use any kind of dried fruit. Cut larger fruit like dried apricots, dates, or figs into smaller pieces.

For cranberry/orange scones: substitute 1/3 cup (45g) dried cranberries for currants (chop up a little if they are really big) and about 1/2 teaspoon of orange zest (orange part only). Err on the side of caution with the zest as orange goes pretty quickly from "this is nice" to "this tastes like paint stripper."

For chocolate hazelnut scones: substitute chopped, toasted hazelnuts for the currants and add 1/4 cup (45g) mini chocolate chips or finely chopped chocolate from a good quality chocolate bar. Skip the sugar on top; make a drizzle instead by gently melting 1/4 cup (60g) chocolate hazelnut spread (look for brands that do not contain palm oil) and Jackson Pollock it over the scones when they come out of the oven.

For cheese scones: Substitute 1/2 cup (118g) grated cheddar (or other sharp) cheese for the currants and add 2 tablespoons of chopped, fresh chives or green onion tops. You can also splash out and add about 1/4 cup (55g) crumbled, very crisp bacon and 1 teaspoon of freshly ground black pepper for a bacon, cheese, and chive version.

For blueberry scones: Substitute 1/2 cup (50g) fresh blueberries for the currants. You can use frozen, but you may need to cut back on the buttermilk a little as the frozen berries will give off a lot of juice. If you can find them, dried blueberries are also great in scones. Add grated zest (yellow part only) of one small to medium lemon. Don't skip the lemon. Blueberries need something to play off or they taste of nothing when they're baked.

Your imagination is the limit here. Except chocolate and orange together. That is not okay.

INDIVIDUAL POTICE

We don't have room at the teahouse to roll out a giant potica dough, and we found that sliced desserts don't look as nice on the tea service. So, with some tweaking and trial and error, we developed these. The recipe is adapted from Betsy Oppenneer's *Celebration Breads*, which should be on the shelf of anyone who enjoys travel through baking. So without the blessing of Vesna's mom or Jože the God of Potica—and with apologies to Eddie Izzard for stealing her joke—here are our nontraditional, sport-sized potice.

For the dough:

2 1/2 teaspoons (7g) active dry yeast (For Americans, at least, this is one packet of yeast.)
2 tablespoons of warm water, 105°-110°F (40°-43°C)
3 large egg yolks, reserve whites for the filling
3/4 cup (175mL) milk
1 teaspoon fine sea salt
1/4 cup (50g) granulated sugar
3 to 4 cups (360g-480g) all-purpose flour
1/2 cup (1 stick/4 ounces/114g) butter, melted

For the filling:

4 cups (460g) walnuts
2 cups (320g) raisins
1/2 cup (120mL) heavy cream, scalded (heated in a pan until tiny bubbles appear at the edge)
1/4 cup (85g) runny honey
1/4 cup (1/2 stick/2 ounces/60g) butter, melted
2 teaspoons cinnamon
3 large egg whites, beaten until stiff peaks form

To serve:

Melted butter

Powdered sugar

In a small bowl or measuring cup, add the warm water and a pinch of the 1/4 cup of sugar and sprinkle the yeast over. Let it froth up a bit to wake up the yeast, about 5 minutes. This also makes sure your yeast beasts aren't dead. Once you've got some bubbling, in a large bowl beat together the egg yolks, milk, salt, sugar, yeast mixture, and two cups (a third to a half of the total amount) of flour.

Stir vigorously with a wooden spoon for 2 to 3 minutes. Drizzle in the butter and stir until incorporated into the dough. Gradually add more flour, about 2 heaping tablespoons at a time, just until the dough comes away from the side of the bowl. Turn it out onto a lightly floured work surface and knead until the dough is smooth and elastic. If you poke it with the end of your finger, it should feel a bit like poking yourself in the cheek, and the dent in the dough (not your face) should spring back slowly.

Place the dough in an oiled bowl (you can use the same mixing bowl, just rub some oil in it) and cover with a tea towel or plate and allow to rise until doubled in size. This should take about an hour but will depend on what "room temperature" is at your house. If it's cold, you can turn the light on in your oven (don't turn the oven on) and let the dough rise in there. The bulb (unless you have an LED) will create just enough heat for a makeshift proofing drawer.

While the yeast are chowing down, make the filling. Grind the walnuts and raisins together in the bowl of a food processor, pulsing until fine. If you don't have a food processor, you can grind them together in a mortar and pestle for an old-fashioned kitchen workout. If you don't have a mortar and pestle, you can just chop them. The texture won't be as smooth, but it will still taste good. Don't let not having kitchen equipment stop you. However you get things done, when you are done, add the walnut-raisin mixture to a large mixing bowl and pour over the scalded cream. Let this sit until the cream is absorbed into the mixture. Add the honey, melted butter, and cinnamon and stir to combine. Fold in the beaten egg whites, cover with a lid or plate, and set aside.

This is where things take a sharp departure from tradition. Say a little prayer that Vesna's mom doesn't haunt us, and generously butter the cups of two standard 12-cup muffin pans and set aside.

Deflate the now doubled dough ball by pulling the sides into the center and dump it out onto a lightly floured work surface. Divide the dough into 24 equal portions (a scale is best for this, but eyeball it if you have to). Keep the portions covered while working with one piece at a time. Flour a thin, tightly woven tea towel and lay it on the counter or a large wooden cutting board. Working quickly and maybe with a friend, use a well floured rolling pin to roll each portion out very thinly into a rectangle. The size isn't as important as the general shape—about twice as long as it is wide—and the thinness. If there's a pattern on your tea towel, you should be able to see it through the dough.

Spread 1/24 of the filling mixture onto your rectangle leaving a 1/2 inch (2cm) gap along one long side. Using the towel to help, roll the dough up starting with the other long side that has filling all the way to edge, ending with the seam on the underside of your roll. Coil this roll into one of the muffin cups, tuck the end under, and repeat with remaining dough, working as quickly as possible.

Cover the filled muffin pans loosely with a clean towel and allow to double in size. How long this rise will take will depend on how long it took you to get all the dough rolled out and how warm the room is, but expect 20–30 minutes at the least. Don't use the oven trick this time, because you'll need to preheat the oven to 325°F (165°C).

When the baby potice have doubled, bake for 15 to 20 minutes or until the tops are just browned and the internal temperature of the bread reaches 190°F (87°C).

Immediately remove from the pan and allow to cool on a wire rack. To serve, brush with melted butter and dust with powdered sugar.

RECIPES FOR THE MIDDLE PLATE
OF THE TEA SERVICE

CUCUMBER SANDWICHES

Cucumber tea sandwiches have a certain reputation for being those impossibly dainty things posh ladies have with their tea. Whatever. They are delicious. You don't have to make a whole tea service to go with them, but a cup of tea does make them perfect. If you want to splash out, you can sub very soft cream cheese for the butter.

1 English (hothouse) cucumber (This is the extra long kind usually wrapped in plastic, but the smaller Lebanese cucumbers make a good substitute.)
Sea salt and ground white pepper to taste
1 loaf white pain de mie or Pullman loaf, thinly sliced (see Pantry)
1/2 cup/1 stick (113g) unsalted butter, softened enough that it won't shred the bread when you butter it

Slice the cucumber as thinly as possible with a mandoline or carefully with a very sharp knife. Lay the slices out on a layer of paper towel, or a very clean tea towel, on a plate or tray in a single layer. Sprinkle with salt and pepper and cover with paper towel or another tea towel. Repeat as necessary, stacking the layers, until all the cucumber slices are laid out and seasoned. Leave to drain for at least 30 minutes at room temperature, or refrigerate for longer.

To make the sandwiches, butter one side of two pieces of bread. Layer cucumber slices, slightly overlapped, on the buttered side of one piece and top with second piece of bread, buttered side in. Trim the crusts and cut sandwiches into triangles. Keep well wrapped until ready to serve to prevent drying out.

CURRIED CHICKEN SALAD TEA SANDWICHES

This is by far the favorite at the teahouse. We sell out every day they are on the menu. The chicken salad is wonderful by itself, served on lettuce, for a gluten-free option. Although chicken salad on lettuce will always be Southern-ladies-who-lunch style to me.

2 boneless chicken breasts, poached, cooled, and chopped into small dice, recipe below
1 small stalk of celery, finely chopped
1 shallot, finely chopped
1/2 cup (85g) dried currants
1/2 cup sliced almonds (50g), toasted
2-3 tablespoons good quality mayonnaise, or sour cream for mayonnaise haters (a.k.a. me)
Madras curry powder to taste, see Pantry
Salt and pepper to taste
2 tablespoons fresh parsley, finely chopped
1 loaf whole wheat pain de mie or Pullman loaf, thinly sliced (see Pantry)
Salted butter, softened

Combine chicken, celery, shallot, currants, almonds, mayonnaise or sour cream, curry powder, and salt and pepper in a medium-sized prep bowl and thoroughly mix to combine. Taste for salt and curry powder and refrigerate until ready to make the sandwiches. The flavor is better if the ingredients can mingle for a couple hours in the fridge.

To make the sandwiches, butter one side of one slice of bread and top with a layer of chicken salad and top with another slice of buttered bread, butter side in, of course. Trim crusts and cut into desired shapes. Keep well wrapped until ready to serve to prevent drying out.

POACHED CHICKEN FOR CURRIED CHICKEN SALAD

2 skinless chicken breasts (bone-in or boneless)
Enough water to cover them in a large sauté pan or skillet
2 coin-sized slices of fresh ginger
1 cinnamon stick
2 bay leaves
1 star anise pod
Sliced green onions (optional)
4-5 black peppercorns

Bring the water and all the spices to a good simmer. Add the chicken breasts and make sure they are covered by the water. Crumple and smooth a circle of parchment (baking) paper big enough to cover the pan, and lay it over the breasts to keep them submerged. If anyone asks you what this piece of baking paper is called when used this way, you can tell them it is often referred to as a drop lid. Return the water to a bare simmer and let poach for about 20 minutes or until the thickest part of the meat reaches 160°F (71°C). The temperature will continue to rise to the recommended safe temperature of 165°F (74°C). Remove from the liquid and allow to cool enough to handle. The broth can be strained and refrigerated or frozen for use later in soups.

And yes, my freezer is often full of weird things that need to get used up.

SOME ASSEMBLY REQUIRED TEA SANDWICHES

SMOKED SALMON TEA SANDWICHES

I'm going to skip amounts for these as you are only assembling and can make as few or as many as you like. At the teahouse we make these on white pain de mie or Pullman bread or in a mix and match style using one slice of white pain de mie and one slice of whole wheat pain de mie *(see Pantry)*. Spread one slice of bread with a layer of cream cheese, a little more thickly than you would spread with butter, and top with a sprinkle of either very finely chopped chives or dill, or a mixture of both. You can also add some whisper thin crescent moons of red onion. Arrange a layer of very thinly sliced cold-smoked salmon (or gravlax) over the cream cheese. Butter the other slice of bread and close up the sandwich. Press the sandwich gently with the flat of your palm to adhere everything without smooshing the bread. Cut off the crusts (cook's treat) and cut into quarters: across into triangles or squares or all one direction to make skinny rectangles. For a fancier presentation with triangles, butter one short side of the triangle and dip into finely chopped chives or dill.

CHEDDAR AND CHUTNEY SANDWICHES

Again, this is an assembly job. There's a recipe for Spiced Apple Chutney in the Pantry section, but you can use commercial chutney, no shame. At the teahouse we make these on whole wheat pain de mie (see Pantry) sliced a little thicker than for most of the other sandwiches. On a buttered slice of bread, lay a thin but not stingy piece of very sharp cheddar cheese and add a good smear of chutney, then top with another piece of buttered bread. Cut into desired shapes.

If your chutney is too chunky, you can put a couple spoonfuls on a clean cutting board and chop through with a knife. Use a dough scraper or spatula to get it off the board to save the blade on your knife. You can also make a more rustic version of this tea sandwich using small, soft brown bread rolls. Split the rolls not quite all the way through and butter each cut side. Tuck in a thicker slice of cheddar and add a spoonful of chutney on top of the cheese.

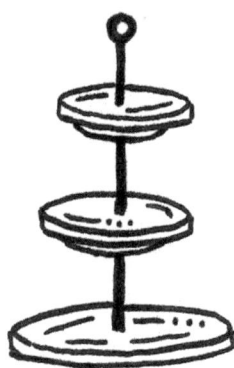

RECIPES FOR THE BOTTOM PLATE
OF THE TEA SERVICE

BURNT-BUTTER CUPCAKES WITH CHOCOLATE GANACHE FROSTING

These were inspired by kitchen queen Nigella Lawson from her book *How to Be a Domestic Goddess*. I appreciate deeply that the book was so named with her tongue firmly in her cheek. I, too, can bake but have yet to be domesticated. These are a particular favorite of Faron's, and I make him a batch for his birthday, even now. You can stretch this to get 12 small cakes, but I usually make 10 so they have a little more substance to balance the ganache.

For the cupcakes:

1/2 cup plus 2 tablespoons (150g) unsalted butter
3/4 cup (125g) cake flour
1 teaspoon baking powder
1/2 teaspoon fine sea salt
3 tablespoons granulated sugar
5 tablespoons, packed, light brown sugar
2 large eggs
1 teaspoon vanilla extract
2-3 tablespoons milk

For the frosting:

4 ounces (115g) semisweet chocolate
4 ounces (115 mL) heavy cream
Large flake sea salt, like Maldon or Cyprus Flake salt

Preheat oven to 400°F and line 10 cups of a 12-cup muffin or cupcake pan with the cupcake papers of your choice.

In a small saucepan, add all of the butter and melt over medium heat. Once the butter is melted, swish it around gently as it bubbles up—this is the water boiling off—and the solids that collect on the bottom start to brown. Keep going until the butter has a toasted nutty smell. You aren't actually burning the butter, but you are going to get those solids to a dark brown. Take off the heat and set aside to cool a bit.

In a large mixing bowl, whisk together the cake flour, baking powder, sea salt, and the white and brown sugars. In a small bowl or measuring cup, whisk together the eggs, vanilla, and milk. Pour the wet ingredients into the dry and pour the browned butter over, scraping all the toasty browned bits into the batter. Whisk until there are no lumps and divide batter among the 10 paper-lined cups. In recipes, you will often be told that you should fill the remaining two cups with water, but that isn't necessary. You would only need to do that if you had buttered or greased the cups and run out of batter. Filling the empty, greased cups in that case would keep the grease from burning.

Bake for 15–20 minutes, until a toothpick inserted into one of the cupcakes tests clean. Cool for about 10 minutes in the pan and then remove onto wire rack to cool completely.

While the cupcakes are cooling, chop the chocolate into small shards and put in a medium-sized, heat-proof bowl. In a small saucepan, heat cream to just before the boil; a few tiny bubbles will appear at the edges of the pan. Pour the hot cream over the chopped chocolate and stir until the chocolate is melted. Let this cool to a thick pouring stage.

Once your cupcakes are cooled to room temperature and your chocolate has cooled to that pouring consistency, spoon a tablespoon of ganache over each cupcake and let it spread out as it chooses with the occasional drip (you may want to put the rack on a baking sheet to catch any errant chocolate). Before the ganache completely sets, sprinkle a tiny pinch of flaky sea salt over the center of each cupcake.

If you have ganache left, you can let it cool completely in the fridge. Scoop out teaspoonfuls and roll them into balls in cocoa-dusted hands. Roll in more cocoa powder or powdered sugar for a few bonus truffles.

JO'S BROWNIES

I would love to take 100 percent of the credit for the awesomeness of these brownies, but the original credit goes to The Barefoot Contessa's Outrageous Brownies. Ina Garten adapted these from another recipe, so it just goes to show you that every cook makes a recipe their own. Honestly, the real secret of brownies is simplicity. You can make cheesecake ones and add all kinds of random things, but brownies—in their dense, dark hearts—live to showcase chocolate.

A few special notes are in order. You'll need a half baking sheet, which is 18 inches by 13 inches by 1 inch (460mm x 330mm x 20mm). Extra-large eggs in the U.S. weigh 2.25 ounces (64g), and large eggs weigh ~2 ounces (57g). So, in theory, you could use seven large eggs and remove half an ounce. It's nitpicky as hell, but this recipe is one of those that needs precision for the very best outcome. If you are less concerned with perfection or don't care to do any math, either use extra-large eggs or use seven large ones and don't worry about it. I would encourage you to only use fair trade chocolate. The chocolate industry is appalling once you start digging, and brownies should definitely not come with a side of child labor and slavery.

3 cups (350g) chopped walnuts, divided (These are also good with pecans, but I really prefer the slight bitterness of walnuts.)
1 pound (450g) unsalted butter
2, 12-ounce (340g) packages semisweet chocolate chips (You can sub bittersweet here if that's your thing; it is often mine.)
2, 4-ounce (113g) 75 percent cocoa solids or higher chocolate bars
6 extra large eggs
3 tablespoons instant espresso powder (Sub instant coffee powder if you can't find the espresso powder.)
2 tablespoons vanilla extract
2 1/4 cups (450g) sugar
1 1/4 cups (170g) all-purpose flour, divided
1 tablespoon baking powder
1 teaspoon fine sea salt

Preheat oven to 350°F (180°C).

Toast walnuts by spreading them out on a baking sheet and baking for 8 to 10 minutes or until they just start to smell toasted. Slide off onto a plate or into a bowl to cool.

Wipe down your baking sheet and let it cool completely, if you only have the one. If you happen to have two, or when that one cools, butter then dust with cocoa powder like you would usually do with flour. The cocoa doesn't release quite as well, but it does prevent a white gummy spot if there's a little too much flour in the corners or something. If you don't have cocoa powder, use all-purpose flour.

In a medium bowl over a pan of simmering water, melt together the butter (cut into tablespoon-sized chunks), one bag of the chocolate chips and both chocolate bars broken into small pieces. If you're brave and careful, you can skip the bowl and do this straight in the pan over low heat by melting all of the butter first then adding the chocolate and staying right with it. Set this aside to cool slightly.

In a large bowl, stir together the eggs, espresso powder, vanilla, and sugar. Don't beat this mixture, as you don't want to incorporate a lot of air. Stir the warm chocolate mixture into the egg mixture and allow the whole thing to cool to room temperature. Don't skip this step. The mixture needs to be cool enough to not melt the remaining chocolate chips when added, and to ensure that shiny, crinkly top on the brownies.

In a smaller bowl, whisk together 1 cup (136g) of flour, the baking powder, and salt. Add this into the cooled chocolate mixture and stir to combine. In the same bowl you used to whisk the dry ingredients together, add the remaining bag of chocolate chips, most of the walnuts (reserving 1/4 to 1/2 cup or 75g), and the remaining 1/4 cup (34g) of flour. Toss this together to cover the chips and walnuts with a coat of flour and add them to the brownie mix, along with any residual flour, and stir just to combine. This dusting will help them stay well distributed in the finished brownies instead of all sinking to the bottom. Pour the mixture into your prepared baking sheet and smooth it out into the corners of the pan. Sprinkle the reserved walnuts over the top of the mixture. It's always nice to announce the ingredients in baked goods, but it seems especially important given the prevalence of tree nut allergies.

Bake for 20 minutes. Open the oven door and knock the pan against the oven shelf to deflate slightly. Bake another 15 minutes. A toothpick should test clean when inserted into the center of the pan— unless you manage to skewer a chocolate chip. But that will look like melted chocolate, not batter. These are really best if not over-baked because that tends to make them cakey, and we are going for fudgy and dense. I understand if you like cake brownies. No, actually I don't. I still respect you, but I don't understand.

Allow to cool completely and refrigerate overnight or for at least four hours. Cut into your desired size. These are fairly decadent so a 2-inch (5cm) square is plenty.

RENEGADE TEA BASIC SHORTBREAD RECIPE

Shortbread cookies are the perfect canvas for flavor. We occasionally make other cookies at the teahouse, but cookies aren't our biggest seller and it's much easier to just play off this original recipe. There are lots of suggestions below to do that. Because the main flavor of the plain shortbreads is butter, this is a case where you should use the best, most flavorful butter you can afford.

5 cups (625g) all-purpose flour
1 1/4 cup (250g) granulated sugar
1/2 teaspoon fine sea salt
1 pound (450g) unsalted butter

Preheat oven to 350°F (180°C).

Sift the flour, sugar, and salt together into a large bowl. Chop the butter into small pieces and begin to work into the dough with clean, ring-free hands. (Trust me on the ring-free part—cleaning dough out of settings is a pain in the ass.) Once the mixture comes together, turn it out onto a lightly floured counter or board and knead until the dough cracks. By that, I mean the dough will crack open when you pull it over while kneading. Use as little flour as possible on the board to keep it from sticking.

Roll the dough out a third to a half inch (1 to 1.5 cm) thick. Cut into desired shapes (squares or circles) and place on baking sheet lined with parchment or a reusable baking liner. To ensure that the shortbreads keep their shape and don't spread on the baking tray, refrigerate the baking tray and the cut-out cookies for at least 15 minutes before baking.

Bake until lightly browned on the edges, usually 8–10 minutes. Ovens vary a great deal, and you'll have to play with the times to get the level of doneness you like. It's important to get a little brown on them though; when underdone, they taste mostly of flour.

Depending on the size and shape you choose, this can make up to 100 cookies.

Variations on a theme:

Pink peppercorn shortbread: Add 2 tablespoons ground pink peppercorns to the flour mixture and stir through before adding the butter. You can change up this amount to your taste. At the teahouse we cut these into 2-inch (5cm) diameter circles and dust the tops with granulated or caster sugar before baking. You can also use a mix of pink, green, and black peppercorns or substitute ground grains of paradise for the peppercorns for a flavor that is reminiscent of cardamom.

Special note: Pink peppercorns are unrelated to common black peppercorns but are the berry of either the Peruvian or Brazilian pepper tree. It is considered an invasive species in the U.S., known colloquially as "Florida holly." As they are related to the cashew family, people with cashew or tree nut allergies can have an anaphylactic reaction to pink peppercorns, and some people experience a rash or other symptoms similar to poison ivy exposure when ingested. Pink peppercorns were banned from import into the U.S. in the 1980s, but the ban has since been lifted. The U.S. Food and Drug Administration does not designate pink peppercorns as "recognized as generally safe" to consume. So, if you or whomever you are cooking for is allergic to tree nuts or extra super allergic to poison ivy, skip the pink peppercorns.

Vanilla bean shortbread: Either substitute vanilla sugar or add the scraped seeds from one fresh vanilla bean pod to the mixture once the butter is mostly worked in and then knead it through. At the teahouse, we cut these into diamond shapes and slather the top with a glaze made of 2 cups (240g) sifted confectioners' or powdered sugar, a couple drops of vanilla extract, and just enough milk to make a spreadable icing. Add a tablespoon of milk at a time until you get there.

Lavender shortbread: Add about a tablespoon of dried lavender buds, crushed up in a mortar and pestle, to the flour mixture and stir through before adding the butter. You can up this amount to your taste, but be aware that many people find overly lavendered baked goods akin to eating soap or body lotion. These are usually cut into 1 inch by 3 inch (2x7cm) bars and glazed with icing similar to the one for vanilla bean shortbread—omit the vanilla and use lemon juice instead of milk to make the glaze. To make them super fancy, you can pipe a little lavender bud on each one with some gently tinted royal icing.

Rose shortbread: Same as for lavender substituting crushed, dried culinary rose petals for lavender and adding 1/2 to 1 teaspoon of rose water once the butter is mostly worked in, with the same caveat that too much rose quickly skids into perfume territory. We usually dust these with white granulated sugar or white edible glitter, if you can get it, before baking. Cut into circles or squares.

Again, your imagination is the limit here, but avoid adding more than 1/2 to 1 teaspoon of liquid to the dough as it will change the texture of the shortbread by changing how the gluten develops.

ROASTED GRAPE VERRINES

A verrine is a small, thickly walled glass container for serving a dish in. You can serve almost anything in a verrine. I think of them as very small sweet or savory parfaits or tasting bites. They make a big impact on a tea tray or tower because they add another element and some height, but they are also great for parties. Tiny shots of tomato soup with a skewered square of toasted cheese sandwich? Absolutely. You don't need to run out and buy verrine glasses; shot glasses or small drinking glasses will work. For dainty tea-time presentation, stick with something that holds under 4 ounces. For a dessert or standalone dish, you could go up to a cup's worth and it will still look elegant. If you are allergic to nuts, see the Note for a savory granola option. The number of servings will depend on what size glasses you use, but this will make six standalone dessert-sized portions.

5 cups (750g) of seedless red or black grapes, stemmed (plus a small handful for garnish)
1 tablespoon extra virgin olive oil
2 tablespoons packed dark brown sugar
2 teaspoons finely chopped fresh lemon thyme, regular thyme, or rosemary, depending on which you prefer (Don't use dried rosemary or you'll be picking what feels like pine needles out of your teeth.)
A grind or two of freshly ground black pepper
2 cups (560g) plain Greek yogurt (You can choose whether to use regular or low fat, but if you want something especially luscious, triple-cream Icelandic yogurt is wonderful here.)
3 tablespoons of runny honey (Use more if you prefer, but the grapes will be very sweet.)
3/4 teaspoon freshly grated nutmeg
1/4 cup (60mL) white wine (see Note)
1/3 cup (34g) toasted walnuts, broken into smaller pieces by hand (You don't want them chopped to dust.)
Fresh mint, for garnish

Preheat your oven to 425°F (220°C) and spread the grapes out on a rimmed cookie sheet and drizzle them with the olive oil. Roll the grapes about to coat, and roast them for about 15 minutes.

Remove the tray from the oven and sprinkle on the brown sugar, chopped herbs, and pepper. Toss gently to coat, and roast another 15 minutes or until the grapes are just starting to burst and release some juice. This may take a little longer if you started with very firm grapes.

While the grapes are roasting, mix the yogurt, honey, and nutmeg together in a small mixing bowl and set aside.

When the grapes are done, remove them from the oven and pour the white wine over and return to the oven for one to two minutes to bubble up the wine and help create a slightly thickened sauce for the grapes. Remove from oven and set aside to cool. If the sauce in the pan seems very thin, you can remove the grapes from the pan with a slotted spoon and set them aside in a bowl. Tip the liquid into a saucepan and reduce over medium-high heat, just until the sauce coats the back of a spoon. Set aside to cool.

When your grapes and sauce are cooled to room temperature, you can assemble your verrines. Set up your glasses and spoon in the grapes and sauce, a couple spoonfuls or about 1/3 of the glass. Try to keep the sides of the glass clean so you don't have streaks in the yogurt layer. Sprinkle in a few walnut pieces and follow up with the yogurt, leaving about 1/2 inch or (1-2cm) of space at the top.

To garnish, slice a few reserved grapes into thin circles and arrange with a piece of walnut (if using) and a tiny mint leaf. If you are using walnuts, I think it's important to include them in the garnish for tea service or parties so folks with nut allergies will know they are included.

Serve with demitasse spoons if you have them. At the very least, make sure your regular teaspoons can get to the bottom of the glass.

Note: If you are serving these as a dessert, the grapes and yogurt can also be served in small bowls. It's your choice to do grapes or yogurt first or kind of nestled side by side. You can use the same garnishes.

If you would like to make an alcohol-free version, reduce honey to 1 tablespoon and substitute unsweetened apple or grape juice for the wine.

Bonus recipe time: Verrines need a little crunch, so if you are allergic to walnuts, don't like them, or want to try something different, give this a go. Feel free to experiment with the seeds: chia, flax, poppyseed, millet, whatever.

4 egg whites
2 teaspoons kosher salt
2 teaspoons ancho chili powder (or to taste)
1 1/2 cups (135g) rolled oats (check for gluten-free, if you need that)
1 cup (130g) raw sunflower seeds
1 cup (160g) unsalted pepitas (hulled pumpkin seeds)
1/4 cup (50g) dark brown (muscavado) sugar

Preheat your oven to 350°F (180°C) and line a baking tray with parchment/baking paper. Combine the egg whites, salt, and ancho chili powder in a medium-sized bowl and whisk until frothy to break up the egg so it sticks to the seeds and oats better. Toss in the remaining ingredients and stir everything together until most everything is coated. Spread out into an even layer on the lined baking tray and bake for 35–40 minutes, giving it a good stir every 10 minutes. Let it cool completely on the sheet before storing in an airtight jar and use up within a week. Use it in the verrines in place of the walnuts, sprinkle it over salads, top your morning oatmeal with it, eat it out of the jar every time you pass it in the kitchen … You get the idea. Makes 2 1/2 cups.

DATE "FUDGE" WITH WALNUTS AND SESAME

We specialize in carbs at the teahouse. I mean, almost everything we serve seems to have flour and sugar or beans in it. But flour can sometimes be an issue for folks, and we like to give people options. This is a great flour-free dessert that can be served on the swankiest of tea trays. It's a variation on a treat found throughout the Middle East and Northern Africa, and though it doesn't contain any added sugar, you will be shocked at how sweet it is. The toasted nuts and sesame seeds go a long way toward cutting through some of that stickiness.

1 1/2 cups (150g) walnut halves
3 tablespoons sesame seeds
1/2 cup (115g) ghee or clarified butter, see Note
1 teaspoon kosher salt
4 cups (900g) pitted dates, coarsely chopped (The soft, sticky medjool dates are best for this.)

Preheat oven to 350°F (180°C) and line a 8 inch by 8 inch (20x20cm) square pan with parchment paper, allowing the paper to hang over on two opposite sides to make a sling so you can easily remove the cooled fudge from the pan to cut it.

Spread the walnuts on a baking sheet and bake for 5 minutes or until lightly toasted. Chop relatively coarsely—you want something around pea-sized. Toast the sesame seeds in a dry frying pan—stirring frequently to avoid scorching—until they have started to take on a golden brown hue and smell toasty.

Melt the ghee or butter in a large, heavy-bottomed saucepan, add the salt and dates, and cook the dates, covered, over low heat for about 10 minutes, stirring frequently until the dates soften into a sticky mass. Using the back of a spoon dipped in cold water, spread half the date mixture over the base of the prepared pan. Sprinkle the walnuts on top and press into the dates. Spread the remaining dates over the walnuts and smooth the surface with wet fingers, pressing down firmly.

Sprinkle with the sesame seeds and press lightly into the dates. When cool, remove the set mixture from the pan and cut into small diamonds or squares to serve.

Note: You can find ghee and clarified butter in most well-stocked grocery stores, or you can easily make them at home. Start by melting unsalted butter in a small saucepan. Use your desired amount of ghee or clarified butter plus 25 percent by weight, or you can make any amount you like, saving some for later, as it keeps very well. Cook over low until bubbling with the occasional sputter. Continue cooking until the foam has mostly evaporated off. Cool slightly and strain through cheese cloth to remove the milk solids that will have settled to the bottom. Refrigerate any leftover clarified butter. You can use it for sautéing because in removing the water and milk solids, you've increased the butterfat's smoke point. If you brown the milk solids in the bottom of the pan before straining the butter, you've made ghee and you didn't have to hand over almost twice the money as you would for the same amount of unsalted butter.

TWICE-BAKED CHOCOLATE SOUFFLÉS WITH POURING CUSTARD

Makes 8

Do not make these when you're in a bad mood, or you'll forget about the whole water bath thing and burn them into a sticky mess. Both recipes can be halved if you're cooking for a smaller crowd. If you want to go full-on decadent, you can add 2-3 ounces (57g-85g) of very good quality dark chocolate, finely chopped, to the custard mix when you add it back to the pan to thicken. Chocolate pouring custard might be addictive, so proceed with caution.

For soufflés:

3 tablespoons (1.5 ounces/40g) unsalted butter
3 tablespoons all-purpose flour
2 tablespoons dark cocoa powder
1 1/4 cups (10 ounces/300mL) whole milk
1/3 cup (68g) granulated sugar
2 teaspoons instant espresso powder (not ground coffee beans)
3.5 ounces (120g) dark chocolate (70% cocoa solids or higher), cut into small chunks
4 large eggs, separated
1 tablespoon vanilla extract
Pinch of fine sea salt

For the custard:

2 1/2 cups (600mL) whole milk
6 large egg yolks (reserve whites for another use)
2 tablespoons vanilla sugar, see Pantry (You can add 1 teaspoon vanilla extract if using regular sugar.)
1 teaspoon plain flour

To garnish:

Seasonal fruit
Additional cocoa powder

Preheat over to 350°F (180°C). Butter eight 2/3 cup (160mL) ramekins and line each with a circle of parchment or baking paper.

To make the soufflés, melt butter in a medium saucepan over low heat and whisk in the flour and cocoa powder to make what is basically a chocolate roux. Slowly drizzle in the milk while whisking to avoid lumps, and stir in the sugar and espresso powder. Continue whisking until thickened.

Take the pan off the heat and add the chocolate. Whisk until melted. Add egg yolks and vanilla and whisk to combine. Set aside.

In a separate bowl, whisk egg whites with a pinch of salt to firm peaks. You can do it by hand, but a hand or stand mixer will be a bit easier.

Spoon about a third of the stiff egg whites into the chocolate mixture and stir through gently to lighten the mixture, then fold in the remaining whites. You don't want streaks of egg white, but you also don't want to deflate all the air you whipped in. Divide the mixture among the ramekins and place them in a large roasting pan or baking dish. Pour boiling water in the pan so that it comes halfway up the ramekins. The safest way to do this is to put the pan with the ramekins in the oven, then pour the water in.

Bake for 17–18 minutes until risen and the tops are starting to crack. Remove from oven and allow to cool.

While the soufflés are cooling, make some custard.

Heat the milk in a medium saucepan just until scalded. Tiny bubbles will appear at the edges of the pan. Set aside.

In a mixing bowl, beat egg yolks with the vanilla sugar and flour until pale and smooth. Slowly drizzle in the hot milk, while whisking, so you don't scramble the eggs. Return the whole mixture to the saucepan and heat very gently, stirring with a wooden spoon, just until the mixture coats the back of the spoon. It will still seem pretty thin, but it will continue to thicken as it cools. I usually pour it through a strainer into the serving jug to remove any scrambled egg bits.

To serve, run a paring knife around the edge of each ramekin and unmold the soufflés by placing a plate on top and inverting the plate and ramekin. Remove the paper rounds from the bottom and transfer to a parchment or baking paper lined tray. Warm in 350°F (180°C) oven for five minutes. Using a wide spatula, remove the soufflés from the tray and plate. Top with a pour of custard and garnish with seasonal fruit or a dusting of cocoa powder.

SOUPS & SAVORIES

VEGETARIAN HARIRA

This was the first soup Fred made when he started working at the teahouse, and it quickly won him the soup maestro title. If we did more than one soup a day, we'd probably serve this one all the time as it is refreshingly bright on a warm day and equally comforting on a cold, gray one.

2 tablespoons olive oil

1 cup (200g) dried chickpeas, soaked in water overnight

1 onion, chopped

8 cups (2L) homemade or low-sodium, store-bought vegetable stock

4 cups (1L) of water

3 cloves of garlic, minced

2 tablespoons finely chopped cilantro, plus 1 tablespoon cilantro, coarsely chopped

Salt, to taste

4 celery stalks, finely chopped

4 ripe tomatoes, peeled and chopped, see Note (can sub a 14.5-ounce or 400mL can of whole tomatoes, chopped with juice)

1 cup (190g) red lentils, sorted and rinsed

1 tablespoon tomato paste

1 tablespoon fresh lemon juice

1/2 teaspoon ground sweet paprika

1/2 teaspoon ground turmeric

1/2 teaspoon ground ginger

1/4 teaspoon ground nutmeg

1/4 teaspoon freshly ground pepper

5 ounces (180g) orzo or vermicelli (broken into small pieces)

1/2 cup (110g) chopped, pitted dates

2 tablespoon coarsely chopped, flat-leaf parsley

1 lemon cut into wedges, to serve

Heat the oil in a Dutch oven or small stock pot over medium-high heat. Add onion and sauté until softened, about 3–5 minutes. Add chickpeas, stock, and water and simmer until chickpeas are softened, about 45 minutes. The chickpeas may take longer depending on their age. Using a mortar and pestle or the flat side of a chef's knife against your cutting board, mash garlic, finely chopped cilantro, and salt into a paste. Add garlic paste, celery, tomatoes, lentils, tomato paste, lemon juice, and spices to pot. Simmer until lentils are tender (red lentils will break down some as they cook), about 25 to 35 minutes. Add pasta and dates and cook, stirring occasionally, until pasta is al dente, about 10 minutes. Stir in coarsely chopped cilantro and flat-leafed parsley. Taste for seasoning and add additional salt and black pepper if needed. Serve in shallow soup plates with lemon wedges and garnish with additional parsley leaves.

You can bulk this up with more vegetables for something more like a vegetable lentil stew. Good choices are sautéed eggplant, zucchini, and red bell pepper cut into medium dice. Cook them separately and add after the pasta is cooked. If you'd like a spicer version, you can swirl through a spoonful or two of Fred's harissa paste (see Pantry).

If you are cooking for one or two people, you can easily halve the recipe or make it as suggested, cooking the pasta separately. Add pasta to individual bowls and keep separate in the fridge to keep the pasta from getting mushy. The version without the added vegetables and with the pasta cooked separately also freezes well.

Note: To easily peel tomatoes, prepare a bowl of water with ice large enough to hold your tomatoes, and put a pan of water on to boil deep enough to submerge at least one of your tomatoes. Cut a small X in the bottom of each tomato and submerge them for 30 seconds in the boiling water, then remove and place in the ice bath. You can start peeling the tomato by placing your paring knife under the flaps of peel where you made the X. It should pull away with light pressure, leaving you with a naked, but otherwise unharmed tomato. If you balk at using all that water to peel tomatoes, let the ice bath and the boiling water come to room temperature and use it to water your plants.

RENEGADE TEA CASSOULET

Fred developed this recipe at the request of Gregor's new beau after poring over J. Kenji López-Alt's *Food Lab*. It's a childhood favorite of Bernard's and makes him a little less homesick. It's now a menu favorite available every Sunday once the weather turns chilly.

Cassoulet is usually made with confit duck legs or quarters and a specialty garlic sausage of the Toulouse region of France. For reasons of food cost and availability, Fred took López-Alt's suggestion, and Renegade Tea cassoulet is made with chicken thighs and local garlic sausages. If you can't find a good garlic sausage locally, kielbasa cut into two-inch chunks makes an acceptable substitute. This is an all day affair, even with the pressure cooker cheat, and it's best reserved for a rainy weekend. Everything cooks into a velvety stew that is the culinary equivalent of a feather duvet and may make you crave rainy fall days perfect for having this for dinner. You will need a 5-6 quart (4.5-4.7L), oven-safe Dutch oven, or if you don't have one, a high-sided casserole with the same capacity will work. You'll just need to transfer the cooked beans and browned meats to it before the oven step. With all the steps and pans, you'll thank yourself for cleaning as you go.

1 pound (450g) cannellini beans (white navy beans can be subbed in a pinch)

Kosher salt

8 ounces (225g) salt pork cut into 3/4-inch cubes (sub cured, American-style bacon, chopped)

1 quart (950mL) chicken or turkey stock

3, 0.25-ounce (7g) packets unflavored gelatin powder (see note for gelatin leaf conversion)

1 large onion, small dice

1 carrot, peeled and cut into three sections

2 celery stalks, cut into 3-inch sections

1 whole head of garlic, top cut off exposing the cloves

4 sprigs of parsley

2 bay leaves

4 cloves (If you are really averse to the thought of finding a whole clove in your stew, sub 1/8 teaspoon ground cloves.)

2 tablespoons duck fat

6 to 8 chicken thighs

Freshly ground black pepper

1 pound (450g) garlic sausage

Stovetop to oven method:

Soak beans overnight with 3 quarts (2.85L) of water and 3 tablespoons of kosher salt.

Measure out stock and sprinkle the gelatin over to let it bloom. (You can omit the gelatin if you are using a homemade stock that set to a jelly when cold.) While that's going on, add salt pork or bacon to a Dutch oven or heavy-bottomed soup pot with a tablespoon of water, and cook over medium heat until browned all over. Remove from the pot with a slotted spoon and either drain or leave on a paper towel. Remove all but 1 tablespoon of pork fat from the pot and add the diced onion. Cook until translucent and softened, scraping up all the browned bits from the pork. Add the drained beans, the cooked pork, carrot, celery, garlic head, parsley sprigs, bay leaves, and cloves and pour the stock/gelatin mixture over. Bring this to a simmer over high heat. Reduce to low and cook until the beans are almost tender but still have some bite. About 45 minutes.

While the beans are cooking, melt the two tablespoons of duck fat in a sauté pan over medium-high heat. Season the chicken on both sides with freshly ground black pepper and a little bit of salt. When the fat is hot, place the chicken thighs, skin-side down, in the fat and cook until nicely browned. The skin should release easily when they are sufficiently browned. Set them aside on a plate. Brown the sausages on two sides in the same pan and set aside.

When the beans are to that tender-but-still-some-bite stage, fish out the carrot, celery, parsley sprigs, and garlic. When the garlic is cool enough to handle, squeeze out all the softened garlic cloves and stir them back into the pot.

Stir the sausage into the beans and nestle the chicken thighs on top with the skin showing. The beans should just be submerged in liquid. If they aren't, add a little water to the pot. Try to leave a little bit of space between the chicken thighs if you have room. Follow the oven directions for the pressure cooker to oven method below.

Pressure cooker/Instant Pot to oven method:

This makes for more dirty dishes but saves soaking the beans and a little bit of time. Measure out the stock and bloom the gelatin as above. If you have a pressure cooker with the sauté function, follow the steps above for cooking the pork and onions, otherwise use a sauté pan to cook the pork and onions in the same order and method and then scrape the onions and all that gorgeous fond (the sticky browned bits you incorporated into the onions) into the pressure cooker and add the cooked pork, carrot, celery, garlic head, parsley sprigs, bay leaves, cloves, and stock/gelatin mixture as above. Following the manufacturer's instructions for your pressure cooker/Instant Pot, cook the beans for 30 minutes with 10 minutes natural pressure release. Release additional pressure according to manufacturer's instructions.

Fish out the carrot, celery, and parsley sprigs as best you can; they will be very soft. Remove the garlic head. When it's cool enough, squeeze out the softened garlic cloves and stir them back into the beans. You have a choice here: the carrots can be mashed and added back to the beans, or you can toss them. I like to mash them and add them back. The celery and parsley are spent and should be tossed.

While the beans are cooking, melt the duck fat in a 5–6 quart (4.5-4.7L) Dutch oven over medium-high heat and season the chicken on both sides with freshly ground black pepper and a little bit of salt. When the fat is hot, put the chicken in, skin side down, and cook until well-browned. The skin will easily release from the pan when it's properly browned. Remove and set aside on a plate. Brown the sausage on two sides and set aside with the chicken. Remove the pan from the heat until the beans are done.

Once the beans are done and you've dealt with the aromatics, add the beans to the Dutch oven you browned the meat in and stir in the sausage. Nestle the chicken thighs on top, skin-side up with a little room between each if you have it. The beans should just be covered with liquid. If they aren't, add a little water to the pot.

To the oven—both methods:

Preheat oven to 300°F (150°C). Bake the cassoulet until a thin crust forms over the top, about two hours. Check occasionally to see if the beans are uncovered and top up the water by pouring some down the inside of the pot, trying not to get the chicken wet or disturb the crust too much.

At the two-hour point, remove the cassoulet from the oven, break the crust with the edge of a spoon and give the pan a shake to redistribute some bean liquid across the top. If at this stage it feels like there is a ton of fat floating on top, you can spoon that off and discard. Whether this happens will depend on how well browned your pork was and/or how fatty the chicken is. Return the pan to the oven and cook for another two and a half hours, breaking the crust and shaking the pan again every half hour. Put in for a final bake until the crust is thick and brown (anywhere from another 30 minutes to an hour). Your total cook time will be between 5 and 6 hours in the oven. Hence the reason to make this on a chilly, rainy day—when having your oven on for that long seems like a pleasant way to warm the kitchen. Serve hot. I don't think it needs anything at all, but a fall salad is nice for some vegetables to counter the meat-palooza you just created. Leftovers are even better, but the chicken skin loses that crackling crispness.

Note: Converting gelatin leaves to powder and vice versa is enough to make reasonable kitchen professionals take up swords against each other. Gelatin powder is a fairly consistent strength across manufacturers, and 1 packet (about 1 tablespoon or 0.25 ounce) is enough to soft set 2 cups of liquid, or about 480mL. Sheet gelatin is sold in different strengths, so you'll need to check the box for instructions to see how much of the sheet gelatin you will need and then do the math. Follow the manufacturer's instructions for softening the gelatin. You'll need to heat up some stock separately to melt the softened sheets before adding them if you are using the pressure cooker method, but they can just be stirred into the beans once everything is hot if you are using the stovetop method.

FRED'S RED LENTILS WITH CARAMELIZED ONIONS

I used to think there was no day so bad that it couldn't be improved by a bowl of this. It's still mostly true, though there are days that are so bad that eating anything seems completely repulsive. If someone you love is faced with one of those days, make this to at least tempt them back to the land of the living.

1 cup (190g) dried red lentils
1/4 cup (50g) fine bulgur wheat
1/4 cup (50g) short-grain, white rice
1 teaspoon sea salt
1 tablespoon freshly ground cumin
2-3 large onions (approximately 1 1/2 pounds or 675g), halved and thinly sliced
1/2 cup (125mL) olive oil
1 tablespoon freshly ground coriander
1 tablespoon ras el hanout, see Pantry
1 teaspoon smoked paprika
Red chili pepper flakes to taste
Salt and freshly ground black pepper to taste

Rinse lentils, bulgur wheat, and rice and let drain. Place the grains and legumes in a deep sauté pan with 1 1/2 quarts of water, cumin, and salt. Bring to a boil, skimming off any foam that rises, and reduce heat to a simmer. Cover and let bubble away for 45 minutes, stirring often to prevent the lentils from sticking to the bottom of the pan and scorching. You may need to add a little water if the lentils start peeking above the surface before they've finished cooking. Red lentils tend to break apart as they cook down.

While the lentils are doing their thing, brown the onions in olive oil over medium-low heat. This may take as long as the lentils take to cook. Patience is definitely a virtue with caramelized onions. Once they are golden brown and smell like culinary heaven, add the ground coriander, ras al hanout, and smoked paprika to the pan and stir through to gently roast (or, more accurately, fry) the spices. Remove the pan from the heat and stir in the chili flakes.

When the lentils are done, add the spiced golden onions to the lentils and stir through. Taste for salt and add a grind or two of black pepper. Serve hot. For fanciness, you can drizzle a spiral of thin, plain yogurt on top and scatter over some chopped cilantro or flat-leaf parsley.

JO'S CHILI AND CORNBREAD

Fred isn't the only one who can make soup/stew magic. My father could throw down a chili and cornbread supper that rivals Aunt Jackie's chicken and dumplings (a recipe she definitely won't part with), so I learned from the best and of course put my own spin on it. If you want to get fancy with the cornbread, you can bake it in a corn stick pan or muffin tin—which we usually do for the teahouse. But a triangle cut from a round, baked crispy-edged in a cast iron skillet, is the original for a reason.

Start with the chili:

2 teaspoons canola or safflower oil

3 or 4 large onions, small dice

1 tablespoon kosher salt, divided

1 pound (450g) ground beef (see note for a vegetarian version)

1 teaspoon freshly ground black pepper

4 large cloves garlic, minced

2 tablespoon Worcestershire sauce

1 tablespoon ground cumin

1 tablespoon ground coriander

3 tablespoons ancho chili powder

1/2 teaspoon cayenne chili powder (more or less to taste)

1, 12-ounce (350mL) bottle of dark beer (a stout, porter or dunkel)

1, 12-ounce (350mL) can of Coke, or other dark cola (Just don't tell me about it. Sometimes you just have to do the thing.)

1, 28-ounce (790g) can fire-roasted crushed tomatoes

1 pound (450g) dry pinto beans, cooked (can sub 4, 14.5-ounce (440g) cans, rinsed and drained)

Heat oil in a soup pot or Dutch oven over medium-high heat. Add onions and 1 teaspoon of the kosher salt. Cook, stirring occasionally, until translucent. In a separate pan—I know, I hate dirtying a thousand pans to make dinner, but our goal is to layer the flavors—cook beef with the remaining salt plus the black pepper until just browned but not caramelized crispy. Drain and add to the onions in the main pot. No more additional dirty dishes for the chili portion. I promise.

To the onion-meat mixture add the garlic, Worcestershire sauce, cumin, coriander, salt, pepper, ancho chili, and cayenne pepper. Stir together to distribute the spice and coat the meat and onions. Cook one to two minutes until spices are fragrant.

Pour in the beer and Coke and simmer for about 10 minutes. The liquid will reduce some but not completely. Add the tomatoes and simmer another 20 minutes. Finally add the beans and simmer a final 30 minutes. If you like really hot chili, you can add a whole habanero pepper to the pot at this point and remove it before serving. Taste for seasoning and add more salt or black pepper if needed. Leftovers will always taste better the next day. My father used to say this was a recipe that required moonlight to make it perfect.

Serve with your choice of toppings and cornbread. Suggested toppings include shredded Cheddar cheese, sliced green onions, sour cream, crumbled tortilla chips, and hot sauce. Jackie always eats hers with crumbled saltine crackers.

While the chili is simmering, make the cornbread:

Cornbread, like chili, is something people love to argue over, as if there were truly a definitive recipe. The definitive recipe is the one you like to make and eat. Dad's original recipe called for two cups of Three Rivers Self-Rising Cornmeal Mix made by White Lily Flour, but it is a regional product and was difficult to find before you could order everything online, so I did the math to make my own mix. I also subbed yellow cornmeal for the white in the Three Rivers mix because I prefer the visual signal of yellow = corn.

1/4 cup (50g) lard or vegetable oil
1 1/4 cups (150g) medium or finely ground yellow cornmeal
3/4 cup (90g) all-purpose flour
2 teaspoons baking powder
1/2 teaspoon baking soda
1/2 teaspoon salt
1 1/4 to 1 1/2 cups (300 to 360mL) buttermilk (thin, plain yogurt will do if you can't get buttermilk)
1 egg, beaten
1/4 cup (50g) sugar

Preheat the oven and your cast-iron skillet with the lard or vegetable oil in it to 425°F.

In a heat-proof bowl—I favor a glass, 8-cup measure for this—whisk together the cornmeal, flour, baking powder, baking soda, and salt. Pour in the buttermilk, egg and sugar and stir together but not completely.

When the pan and oil or lard is hot, remove it from the oven and carefully swirl the fat around to coat the sides of the pan, then pour the hot fat into the cornbread batter and stir to completely incorporate. There shouldn't be any dry bits, but don't over-mix it.

Pour the batter back into the pan, smooth it out a bit, and bake for about 20 minutes or until the top is flecked golden brown and the edges are a darker golden brown. Allow to cool 10 minutes before covering the pan with a serving plate and turning the whole thing over. Or, just serve the cornbread from the skillet while it's hot. Unlike the chili, this is best eaten the same day you make it.

You can add mix-ins, like fresh corn kernels, chopped jalapeños, crumbled bacon or cracklings, cooked pinto beans, chives, etc. Though I am a bit of a purist, you can definitely make your cornbread yours.

Vegetarian chili:

A straight sub with some kind of fake meat product is fine but never quite tastes as good. This version includes more veggies and highlights the bean and tomato flavors. I don't add carrots, though they seem to be the most ubiquitous ingredient in vegetarian chilis. I think they make it too sweet. Amusing, I know, from the woman who puts a can of Coke in her meat chili, but trust me on this.

1 tablespoon canola or safflower oil

2 large onions, chopped (about 4 cups of onion total)

2 teaspoons salt

1/2 pound (250g) cremini or portabella mushrooms, chopped fine (optional)

5 cloves of garlic, minced

1 red or yellow bell pepper

3 tablespoons ground cumin

2 tablespoons ground coriander

3 tablespoons ancho chili powder (since I buy Kashmiri chili in bulk, I sometimes go half ancho, half Kashmiri here)

1/2 teaspoon cayenne chili powder (more or less to taste)

2 tablespoons vegetarian Worcestershire sauce (Annie's brand in the U.S.)

1, 28-ounce (793g) can crushed fire-roasted tomatoes

5 sun-dried tomato halves, soaked in boiling water until softened and minced

1, 15-ounce (425g) can refried beans

1, 15-ounce (425g) can pinto beans, rinsed and drained

1, 15-ounce (425g) can black beans, rinsed and drained

1, 15-ounce (425g) can kidney beans, rinsed and drained

In a Dutch oven or heavy soup pot, heat oil and sauté onions with the salt until just starting to brown. Add chopped mushrooms and sauté until they release their liquid and it evaporates. Add the garlic and bell pepper and cook just until softened. Add cumin, coriander, chili powders, and Worcestershire sauce and sauté a minute or two to coat the vegetables in the spices. Add crushed and sun-dried tomatoes and simmer for 20 minutes. Add beans and simmer until warmed through. If the chili is too thick, thin with vegetable stock or water. Taste for seasoning and serve hot with desired toppings and cornbread. This is also suitable for vegans without the cornbread and with vegan toppings, of course.

MINESTRONE MAJA

The original minestrone recipe is based on borlotti bean broth. Maja updated it for the teahouse with her herb bombs and pasta rather than the more traditional rice, and we've kept her version in rotation on the menu since. Cook the pasta separately and store leftovers separately so the pasta doesn't swell up and absorb all the broth. The potatoes can also be omitted if you don't want to do carbs on carbs. The Parmesan rind adds a meaty, umami flavor to the broth, but it can be omitted for a vegan version or if you don't have a slightly embarrassingly large stash of Parm rinds in your freezer. This is a great soup to clean out the veg drawer with, so feel free to add what you have on hand. Add anything in the cabbage family—cauliflower, broccoli, rapini, etc.—the same time the cabbage goes in so they don't overcook and smell like old, dirty socks.

2 tablespoons extra virgin olive oil

3 cloves of garlic, minced

1 medium onion, chopped

3 small to medium carrots, peeled and chopped

3 medium waxy potatoes (Yukon gold or red bliss), peeled and chopped

1 cup dried borlotti beans (substitute: pinto or red kidney beans)

1, 28-ounce (~800g) can San Marzano tomatoes, chopped, reserving juice

3 tablespoon good-quality tomato paste

1 Parmigiano-Reggiano rind

2 bay leaves

3 or 4 thick parsley stems, leaves removed

Salt and fresh ground black pepper to taste

2 cups fresh (in-season) or frozen peas

1 small head Savoy cabbage, halved, cored and finely sliced

1 herb bomb, depending on size (see Pantry)

2 cups orecchiette, cooked and held separately
Parmigiano-Reggiano, for serving

In a Dutch oven or large soup pot, heat olive oil and add garlic, onions, carrots, and potatoes. Sauté for one to two minutes, until you can smell the garlic. To this vegetable mixture, add dried beans, tomatoes and their juice, the tomato paste, the Parmesan rind, bay leaves, and parsley stems. Add 8 cups of water, see Note, to the mix and bring to a boil. Reduce heat, cover, and allow to bubble away on a slow simmer for 2 hours, stirring occasionally.

When the beans are mostly done—you can check by sampling a bean or three—add the cabbage and peas and simmer another 15 minutes with the lid off. You can cook the pasta in this last 15 minutes if you haven't already done so. At the end of the 15 minutes, drop in the herb bomb and let it melt before stirring through. If you don't have ready-made herb bombs, chop up about a 1/2 packed cup (~25g) total fresh parsley, basil, and a little sage and/or oregano and stir that through instead. Taste for seasoning.

To serve, add a spoonful of orecchiette to each bowl and ladle the soup over. Garnish with a few flakes of Parmesan shaved off with a vegetable peeler and arrange on top. An odd number always looks a little nicer.

Note: You can also use vegetable or chicken stock (if you aren't serving vegetarians) to boost the flavor.

LEMONY CHICKPEA AND OLIVE STEW

I'm not going to lie, this seems like a lot of work—faffing about with multiple pans and cooking forever. The goal is to layer the flavors, and it's so worth it. I promise. The teahouse smells like heaven when Fred is making this, and almost everyone who comes in orders it when it's on the menu. You can make this as spicy as you like, but we usually keep it to one-alarm and offer folks a pot of harissa if they want it hotter.

1/2 pound (230g) dried chickpeas (can substitute 2 15-ounce cans of prepared chickpeas)
1/2 cup (120mL) olive oil, divided
2 large yellow onions, peeled and chopped
2 tablespoons tomato paste
1 teaspoon rose harissa (see Pantry)
4 garlic cloves, crushed
2 small eggplant, unpeeled, diced into 1/2" cubes
3 or 4 small preserved lemons or 1 to 2 large ones (see Pantry)
1/2 cup (90g) Moroccan or other oil-cured black olives
1 tablespoon flat-leaf parsley, chopped
1 tablespoon fresh mint, chopped

Soak the chickpeas for 24 hours in cold water if using dried. Drain and place in a pan with enough water to cover by an inch and a half. Bring to the boil then simmer 1 1/2 to 2 hours until chickpeas are tender. When cooked, drain and reserve cooking water. If you have a pressure cooker, you can also cook them without soaking, following the manufacturer's recommendations for beans.

Heat half the oil in a large sauté pan or sauteuse pan (fancy word for a sauté pan with two loop handles instead of one long handle), and sauté the onions for 10 minutes or until softened and slightly golden. Add tomato paste, harissa, and garlic and cook for another 30 minutes over a very gentle heat, stirring occasionally. In a separate sauté pan (sorry, but necessary here), heat the remaining olive oil and fry the eggplant until nicely browned. Transfer the fried eggplant into the pan with the onions and cook an additional 30 minutes or until the eggplant is meltingly tender.

Add the chickpeas and whole preserved lemons along with the olives to the simmering onion and tomato paste mixture. Add enough of the chickpea cooking water to give everything a wet texture and simmer an additional 30 minutes, tasting for seasoning, keeping in mind the preserved lemons and olives are salty and will season the broth as it cooks.

Remove the lemons and quarter them. Remove and discard the flesh and cut the peel into thin strips. Taste for seasoning one last time. Then, stir the chopped herbs into the pot and scatter the lemon peel over the top.

Note: There are recipes for regular and rose harissa, as well as preserved lemons, in the Pantry section, but harissa and preserved lemons can be purchased in most Middle Eastern grocery stores or ordered online. You can substitute regular harissa for rose, if it's unavailable. Commercially available preserved lemons tend to be quite small. Homemade ones will be much larger, hence the difference in the recommended amounts.

GAZPACHO DORADO

Gazpacho is one of those things that frankly sounds like it would be a train wreck when you read through the recipe. In reality, it transcends the sum of its parts. This version tosses the usual tomatoes aside for a cornucopia of autumn vegetables. If you can't find absolutely everything called for in the recipe, it will still be good. The flavor varies a little every time, depending on the exact size of the veg you use. You may find you like it better with more or less of some vegetables. We serve this as a bowl of soup at room temperature garnished with roasted baby vegetables and a sprinkling of smoked paprika. But we also serve it as a soup shooter with the savory course of a full tea. If it's too thick for shot glasses, you can thin it with more stock. I've even added some vodka for a Gilded Mary, though it's better as a shooter than a long drink and requires very good vodka. Or, more accurately, I require very good vodka. However you make or serve it, this soup's sunny hue has a mood lifting quality that is always welcome. Father Peter comes by every time it's on the menu. Like Fred, he developed an ultra-sensitive type of psychoscopy—but only by taste. He likes to regale the regulars with a rundown of where every vegetable was grown and how it made it to our kitchen.

2 cloves garlic, minced

1/2 medium yellow onion, roughly chopped

1 medium carrot, peeled and roughly chopped

1/2 small bulb of fresh fennel, roughly chopped (reserve fronds)

1 small golden beet, peeled and roughly chopped (Don't substitute a
red beet unless you want to make Gazpacho Rosado Sucio instead.)

1 small turnip, scrubbed and roughly chopped

1 medium parsnip, peeled and roughly chopped

1/4 head Savoy cabbage, roughly chopped

1 leek, cleaned and white part only roughly chopped (reserve green
part for stocks)

1 small acorn squash, cut in quarters, seeds removed (can sub one
small butternut squash peeled and roughly chopped)

1 small celeriac (celery root), peeled and roughly chopped (You can
sub two large stalks of celery, but add 1/4 teaspoon of celery seed to
the spices.)

1 teaspoon ground cumin

1 teaspoon ground turmeric

1 teaspoon ground ginger

1 teaspoon ground white pepper

1/2 teaspoon cayenne pepper (or to taste)

1/2 cup (125mL) olive oil, divided

1/2 cup (75g) blanched, whole almonds, roughly chopped

2 slices day-old, country-style bread, roughly chopped

1/4 cup (40g) golden raisins (You can sub dark ones if you don't want
the extra sulfites, but they will change the final color a little bit.)

4 cups (1L) unsalted or low-sodium chicken stock (You can substitute
golden vegetable stock for a vegan/vegetarian version.)

1 tablespoon large flake kosher salt

1 teaspoon freshly ground black pepper

Chopped green onions (scallions), for garnish

Finely chopped reserved fennel fronds, for garnish

Smoked paprika, for garnish

Preheat oven to a blazing 425°F (220°C).

In a large bowl, combine the garlic and all the chopped vegetables. Mix the spices (down to cayenne) together in a small bowl. Add the mixed spices and half of the olive oil to the vegetables, stirring and tossing to thoroughly coat the vegetables with the oil and spice mixture.

Spread the vegetables out on a baking sheet in a single layer and roast for about 30 minutes, turning frequently and removing any vegetables before they char. You can set them aside in your original mixing bowl.

Remove all vegetables from the oven and let them cool. Once cooled, you can scrape the flesh from the acorn squash, if using, and discard the skins. Add cooled vegetables, bread, almonds, and raisins to the jar of a blender and puree until smooth. If your vegetables are still warm, remove the center of the blender lid to avoid any trapped steam exploding out and painting you and your kitchen in yellow soup. If the mixture is too dry for the blender, add about 1/4 cup of the stock to get things going. Once you have a smooth puree, slowly drizzle in the remaining 1/4 cup of olive oil with the motor running. You may need to do this in batches depending on the size of your blender.

Pour the gazpacho into a large, clean bowl and add the stock. Taste for salt and pepper, and pour into double shot glasses and garnish with finely sliced green onions, a fennel frond and a sprinkling of smoked paprika for tea service. For a meal, serve in bowls and garnish with roasted baby vegetables, sliced green onions, a pinch of fennel fronds and the sprinkling of smoked paprika. It's best eaten the same day.

VEGETABLE TORTA

This makes a great showy brunch dish, but it is filling enough for a weeknight dinner if you have a little extra time for some kitchen meditation or don't mind eating a little later than usual. At the teahouse, we serve this with a seasonal green salad and sometimes substitute other roasted vegetables for the potatoes. You can also add some dill with the fresh herbs in the custard, if you're into that.

For the veg:

1 medium to large head of garlic, outer papery skins removed and the top third cut off, exposing the flesh inside
3 to 4 medium-sized waxy potatoes, boiled whole, cooled and sliced into 1/4-inch (a teeny bit more than 0.5cm) thick slices
2 medium red or orange bell peppers, cut into quarters, stems and seeds removed
8 ounces (250kg) cremini or brown button mushrooms, sliced
2 medium onions, halved and sliced thinly
3 tablespoons olive oil, divided

For the custard:

4 oz. (115g) cream cheese, room temperature
6 large eggs
1/4 cup (60mL) heavy cream
2 tablespoons fresh basil, torn (substitute 1/2 teaspoon dried basil)
2 teaspoons fresh thyme, leaves stripped from the stem (1/2 teaspoon dried thyme)
2 teaspoons freshly squeezed lemon juice
Salt and pepper to taste, keeping in mind the vegetables will be lightly salted and the cheese will be salty, and also that under-salted eggs are a serious disappointment.

Assembly:

3 ounces (90g) Asiago cheese, finely grated, more if you want

To serve:

10-12 basil leaves, rolled together and sliced into thin ribbons

Preheat oven to 450°F (230°C) and line a baking sheet with parchment or baking paper.

For the garlic, make a doubled square of aluminum foil, place the garlic in the center and drizzle with 2 teaspoons of olive oil. Wrap it up, sealing to avoid olive oil drips in your oven, and place directly on the rack. You can get this started while you prep the other vegetables.

Arrange the bell pepper quarters and onion slices on the baking sheet, peppers on one side and onions on the other. Brush with olive oil and sprinkle with salt and pepper. Roast until vegetables are softened and browned, about 35 minutes, turning the pan around in the oven about halfway through and removing any of the onions that seem to be getting too dark. The bell pepper skins should get pretty blistered and charred.

While the vegetables are roasting, sauté the sliced mushrooms in olive oil, sprinkled with a little salt. Cook until the mushrooms have given up their liquid and it has evaporated from the pan. Set aside to cool.

Remove the browned veg from the oven and transfer the peppers to a small bowl and cover with a plate to allow them to steam. This will make it easier to peel the skins off when they are cooled enough to handle. Continue to roast the garlic another 10-15 minutes or until it is very soft and golden brown. You can check it by giving the packet a squeeze (using an oven mitt or tea towel, please). Set aside to cool.

Reduce oven to 375°F (190°C). Thoroughly butter a 9-inch (22cm) springform or removable bottom, high-sided cake pan and line the bottom with a circle of parchment or baking paper. Butter the paper too.

For the custard, add softened cream cheese, eggs, cream, fresh herbs, lemon juice, salt, and pepper to the bowl of a food processor. Squeeze the roasted garlic cloves out of their skins and add to the bowl. Process by pulsing until combined. You can do this by hand if necessary, but start by mixing the cream cheese and garlic together before adding one egg at a time to get a smooth mixture, then stir in the other ingredients.

On to assembly: Start with a layer of potato slices, nestling them fairly close together with a little bit of room in between for the egg to find its way to the bottom of the pan. None of the vegetable layers needs to fully cover the pan; you want those gaps for the custard. Sprinkle with a little bit of cheese. Add a layer of bell pepper (skins removed) and sprinkle with cheese and top with a layer of mixed onions and mushrooms. Pour half the custard over and tilt the pan around to let the egg mixture settle into the gaps. Repeat layers with remaining vegetables and custard. Top with more grated cheese and bake until the top is lightly browned and the center is set or the internal temperature is 175°F (80°C), 30 to 45 minutes, start checking at 30.

Once out of the oven, allow to stand at least 20 minutes. Run a thin spatula or paring knife around the edge and remove the ring or outer pan. Slice and scatter with basil to serve. Can be served warm, room temperature, or cold.

THE RENEGADE TEA PANTRY

Punk rock is based on a DIY aesthetic, and our approach to food is no different. Everything in this section with the exception of Maja's herb bombs can easily be purchased at your regular grocery store or ordered online, but we prefer to make what we can ourselves because we have total control over the quality of the ingredients and because we're nerds who are willing to give any recipe a shot at least once.

EASY PAIN DE MIE, A.K.A. PULLMAN LOAF

For the most geometrically pleasing tea sandwiches possible

This is best made in a stand mixer, but you can do it by hand. Start out with a trusty wooden spoon, then switch to hand kneading. You will need a 9-inch (23cm) Pullman loaf pan that has a lid to prevent the bread from making that domed top and ensure a tighter crumb. That tighter crumb makes it easier to slice the bread really thinly. You can make it in a regular standard loaf pan covered with two layers of aluminum foil firmly wrapped around the pan. (Remember to butter the foil where the bread will touch it.) You could also skip the lid part all together; you will get a domed top that you'll have to cut off for that geometric near perfection in your cut sandwiches, but it will still taste good. If you want to skip making the bread altogether, in the U.S., at least, Pepperidge Farm has a Very Thin White—honestly, the jokes write themselves—and a Very Thin 100% Whole Wheat that you can use instead. But, finally, if you don't want to make the bread and you don't want to give Big Bread your money, use whatever bread you want, leave the crusts on, cut them with owl-shaped cookie cutters. Tea sandwich anarchy could be more than a great band name.

1 cup (240g) warm water, 110°F (43°C)
3 tablespoons (28g) dry milk powder (If you don't have dry milk powder, substitute 1 cup of warmed milk for the warm water.)
5 teaspoons (14g) instant yeast (This is two packets of yeast.)
3 tablespoons (39g) sugar
1/4 cup (53g) light oil, like safflower or canola
1 1/4 teaspoon (7g) salt
1 large egg (approximately 60g), room temperature, beaten
4 1/4 cups (535g) all purpose flour

In the bowl of a stand mixer not yet snapped into the mixer, combine warm water and milk powder and let cool to 80°F (27°C), then add yeast and sugar. Mix well and let sit until yeast gets frothy.

Snap the bowl in place with the flat beater attachment. Add oil, salt and beaten egg and mix.

Add flour and, continuing with the flat beater attachment, mix on low speed for 4 to 5 minutes. Change to the dough hook attachment and knead for 7 minutes. The dough should still be tacky.

Dump the dough out onto a very lightly floured work surface and hand knead a few times to bring the dough together. Form it into a ball by tucking the dough under until you have a smooth top. Leave the dough on your work surface and cover with the inverted mixing bowl for about 15 mins to let the gluten relax a bit.

Remove the bowl and knead the dough lightly to gently deflate the air pockets. Roll out the dough with a very lightly floured rolling pin to a rectangle just shy of the length of your Pullman pan and about two and half times as wide. Roll that rectangle into a log from the long side and place the log, seam-side down, in your lightly greased Pullman pan (don't forget to grease the lid but don't put it on yet) and place in your oven and turn the light on but don't turn on the oven. The bulb creates enough heat to fake a proofing drawer, unless you have an LED in your oven.

Watch until the dough is about 1 inch from the top of the pan and remove from oven. Place or slide the lid on the pan and leave the pan in a warm place while you heat the oven to 375°F (190°C).

Bake with the lid on for 30 minutes. The bread is done when the internal temperature is 200°F (93°C). Turn out the bread immediately onto a rack and cover with a dish towel. Allow to cool completely before slicing. It's tough to wait, but bread continues the cooking process as it cools. Cutting into it too early can make the bread gummy.

For a whole wheat version:

Swap out 2 cups of the all-purpose flour with whole wheat flour and swap out the remaining all-purpose flour for bread flour (strong flour in British terms) to give the bread a better structure.

The night before you want to make the bread, mix the whole wheat flour with 3/4 cup of the water. This will hydrate the very thirsty whole grain flour.

Swap honey for the sugar and reduce the yeast to 3 teaspoons.

Allow the dough to completely double in size on that first resting period, so 45 minutes to an hour depending on how warm your kitchen is, instead of the quick nap under the bowl the white flour version gets.

When you are ready to mix the dough, follow the same order as for white but add the soaked whole wheat flour with the eggs, then add the remaining flour. Add an extra minute to the kneading time with the dough hook.

Follow the shaping, second proofing, and baking instructions the same as for the white bread.

SPICED APPLE CHUTNEY

Makes ~10 pints (~10 1/2 liters)

If you haven't canned before, in the U.S., I recommend checking out the most recent edition of the yearly *Blue Book* published by Ball or information from your local Extension service available online. Please check local sources of canning information in your country or location, especially in relation to altitude adjustments for processing time. I'm going to be a mother hen here and say that following proper canning procedure is really important. If you find that any of your stored chutney has come unsealed in storage or smells or looks odd when you open it, throw it out. It is always better to be safe than sorry. Store opened jars in the fridge and use up within a month.

If you can't imagine getting through 10 pints of chutney in a year, you can halve or quarter this recipe with no issues. I also recommend packing these smaller batches in half pints with 1/4 inch (.5cm) headspace if you have a small household; it's hard to get through a pint of chutney by yourself before it goes moldy in the fridge. If you can't fit all the jars in your water bath at the same time, you can process in batches. Keep the remaining chutney and jars warm while the first batch processes.

10 to 12 medium-sized apples, peeled, cored, and chopped into small dice (2 pounds or ~1kg after coring, peeling and chopping)

1 cup (150g) yellow onion, chopped

1 cup (150g) red bell pepper, chopped

2 lbs. (1kg) raisins

3 tablespoons yellow mustard seeds (or a mix of black and yellow)

2 tablespoons ground ginger

2 teaspoons allspice, whole

2 teaspoons Madras curry powder, see recipe in this section

2 teaspoons pickling salt (fine salt without any anti-caking additives, can use fine sea salt)

2 small red, hot peppers, seeded and minced (keep your heat preference in mind)

1 clove garlic, minced

4 cups (750g) dark brown sugar, packed

4 cups (1L) apple cider vinegar, 5% acidity or higher

Prepare your canning setup, including water bath, and sterilize 10 pint or 1/2 liter jars and lids.

Add all ingredients to a large, heavy-bottomed pot. Bring to a boil, reduce heat and simmer uncovered until thick. Stir frequently to avoid scorching. This may take anywhere from 45 to 60 minutes, depending on the variety and juiciness of the apples used. The mixture will also thicken as it cools.

Ladle hot chutney into hot, sterilized pint (.5L) jars leaving 1/2 inch (1cm) headspace. Use a plastic or wooden spoon handle to get out all the air bubbles. Check the headspace again and adjust if necessary. Wipe jar rims and put the lids on. Process in a boiling water bath for 10-12 minutes (again check local recommendations for processing times based on the jar system you are using and your altitude).

Remove jars to a towel-covered work surface and allow to cool before checking seals. Label with contents and date and allow flavors to develop for about a month before using. Use within a year of canning (this may vary slightly depending on the type of jars you are using).

If you end up with a jar that didn't seal or a jar that wasn't full enough to process, store airtight in the refrigerator and use within two months.

APPLE BUTTER

This is what Southern-style American biscuits dream of. It's perfectly spiced, for me, but you may find you want to adjust or play around with the spices after the first batch. We make it for the teahouse, but I always keep a stash in my flat too. I've addicted many a friend and friend-with-benefits to it. I always think of apple butter and apple chutney as siblings; apple butter's sweet spiced depths to apple chutney's heat and tang. Different applications for different situations, equally good. This recipe can be easily halved, but why?

6 pounds (2.75kg) unpeeled apples, rinsed, stemmed, cored and cut into quarters
1 cup (200g) packed dark brown (muscavado) sugar
2 cups (430g) granulated sugar
2 teaspoons ground cinnamon
1/4 teaspoon ground allspice
1/2 teaspoon kosher salt
1 1/2 cups (355mL) apple juice
1/2 cup (118g) apple cider

Lug out your slow cooker or an electric pressure cooker with a slow cook option—7 quart capacity at least—and add all of your ingredients to the pot. Give everything a good stir to distribute the sugar and spices. Cook this covered, on low, for 20 hours. Yes. 20 hours. This is the complicating factor of trying to do it on the stove. You can make it in the oven though. Add all your ingredients to a non-reactive heavy pan, like an enameled cast-iron dutch oven and plonk in the oven at 200°F (93°C) and follow the directions the same. I honestly don't recommend this for gas ovens though, just because I have a horror of leaving a gas oven on for 24 hours total. Your mileage may vary. After about four hours give the mixture the occasional stir. This is more important in the slow cooker.

However you make it, your house will smell amazing. Who needs potpourri when you have spiced apples? At the 20 hour mark, use a stick blender to puree the apples into a smooth mixture. If you don't have a stick blender, you can scrape everything into a regular blender, best in batches, remembering to remove the circular bit in the middle so steam doesn't build up and blow the lid off. Hot apple butter is the culinary equivalent of napalm; it sticks and it burns. Handle accordingly.

Once it's pureed (and back in the pot if you went the blender jar route), cook on low for an additional four hours. If your apples were particularly juicy, it may take a bit longer. You're going for a dark mahogany color and a consistency that will keep its shape a bit when you run a spoon through.

If you are going to burn through this, you can just ladle into jars and keep stashed in the fridge. If you'd like to keep it for longer, can it. Ladle it into hot sterilized jars with a 1/4-inch headspace and process in a water bath for 15 minutes (depending on your elevation above sea level). As with the apple chutney, please follow your local health and safety guidelines for canning. The canned apple butter will keep up to a year in a cool dark place, and the full recipe makes about 5 pints (about 2.3L total).

HOUSE-MADE HARISSA PASTE
WITH ROSE VARIANT

If you absolutely can't find harissa, don't want to make it, or can't find the ingredients to make it, you can substitute other garlicky chili pastes (sriracha, gochujang, sambal oelek) and your dish will still taste great. I've even tossed in a chipotle in adobo smushed up with some garlic when there's nothing else to be had. Remember: the purpose of cooking is to get tasty food on the table, not to stress the cook out to the point of distraction. It is totally okay to make do, and you often discover something you like better along the way.

15 dried chiles de árbol
2 dried guajillo chiles
1 dried ancho chile
1 tablespoon cumin seeds
1 1/2 teaspoons coriander seeds
3 garlic cloves, smashed
2 tablespoons fresh lemon juice
1 tablespoon white wine vinegar
1 tablespoon tomato paste
1 1/2 teaspoons hot, smoked paprika
1 teaspoon kosher salt
3/4 cup (180mL) olive oil, divided

Place dried chiles in a large heatproof measuring cup or glass bowl and pour boiling water over to cover. Pop a plate on top to hold the heat in and let sit until the chiles are softened and cool enough to handle, 20 minutes-ish. Drain off the soaking water. Remove the stems and scrape out the seeds. You may want to wear gloves if you have them or coat your fingers in oil before handling the chiles, especially if you wear contact lenses.

Toast cumin and coriander in a small, dry skillet over medium-low heat, tossing constantly, until very fragrant, about 3 minutes.

Add the toasted spices to the bowl of a food processor, add the garlic, and pulse until spices are broken up and the garlic is broken down. Add the soaked chiles and pulse until it all comes together into a coarse paste. Add lemon juice, vinegar, tomato paste, paprika, and salt and process until mostly smooth but mixture still has a little texture. With the motor running, stream in 1/2 cup oil.

Scoop out your lovely harissa paste into a jar or other glass storage container and top with the remaining olive oil. This will keep in the fridge for at least a month, but you'll probably find ways to use it up pretty quickly.

For rose harissa: Follow the same procedure but add 1/2 teaspoon caraway seeds with the coriander and cumin for toasting and add 1 teaspoon culinary dried rose petals and 1/4 teaspoon rosewater when you add everything else to the food processor.

HOUSE MADRAS-STYLE CURRY BLEND

This is a basic Madras blend made with easy to source ingredients found in almost every grocery. If you have access to a broader range of spices, you can make the amped up version mentioned in the directions.

8 tablespoons coriander seeds
6 tablespoons cumin seeds
1 tablespoon black mustard seeds (these are smaller than yellow mustard seeds and are often a very dark brown, sub with yellow if you have to)
1 tablespoon fennel seeds
4 tablespoons ground cinnamon
8 tablespoons black peppercorns
1 tablespoon ground nutmeg (freshly ground if at all possible; there really is a huge difference)
1 tablespoon whole cloves
2 tablespoons ground cardamom
2 tablespoons ground turmeric
2 tablespoons ground ginger
1 tablespoon cayenne pepper (less if you want a milder curry)

In a dry skillet over very low heat, toast the seeds until they begin to pop. Once it seems like about half the seeds have popped, add the remaining ingredients. Continue to heat and stir gently until the mixture is quite hot but not burnt. Turn out onto a plate to cool completely before grinding in a spice grinder (a dedicated, bladed coffee grinder works great for this, just don't grind coffee in it) or blender. Once you have a fine powder, store in a jar with a tightly fitting lid and use up within three months for best flavor.

If you have access to a good spice store or don't mind sourcing stuff online, you can up the flavor of your curry powder. To your mixture you can add fenugreek seeds (about 2 tablespoons). Fenugreek has an almost maple-like aroma and adds a lot to the mixture. You can also add dried curry leaves (about 12) to the mixture. Now for the substitutions. Instead of using cardamom powder, substitute 15 green cardamom pods, cracked open by bashing them with the bottom of the spice jar. You can also substitute one whole Ceylon cinnamon stick for the ground cinnamon. Ceylon is the true cinnamon, and the cinnamon stick can be easily broken by hand. The thicker curls of bark are cassia and aren't what we're looking for here. You can also sub 8 Indian long peppers or pipli for the peppercorn. And finally you can substitute Kashmiri chili powder for the cayenne. For your amped up version, toast the fenugreek, cracked cardamom pods, long peppers, and broken up cinnamon stick with the seeds.

Whether you make the first version or the amped up version, feel free to substitute, add, or leave out things to make it your own. There are as many curry blends in India as there are cooks. It's also important to note that Madras changed its official name to Chennai in 1996. So you can also call this Chennai-style curry. There's some evidence that this particular blend owes its origins to London rather than India, but it was still a reflection of the hot curries of Madras, now Chennai.

RAS AL HANOUT

This North African spice blend translates literally to "head of the shop" but more accurately to "top shelf." Every spice trader has their own blend, some including as many as 50 spices. This is a more restrained version that can be achieved with spices easily available. Do use whole spices if at all possible, but even pre-ground ones will give you a haunting depth of flavor in the dishes seasoned with it. It's commonly used to season soups and stews, or what could be called North African curries. It also makes for amazing roast chicken or lamb burgers and can elevate humble roasted vegetables to "head of the table."

To the blend suggested, you can also add any or all of the following: dried culinary rose petals, saffron, mace, lavender, or fennel seeds. Toast the fennel seeds, but just add the others to the grinder with the toasted spices.

2 teaspoons coriander seed
1 teaspoon allspice, whole
1/2 stick Ceylon cinnamon, crumbled (the harder Cassia sticks won't work here, use 2 teaspoons ground cinnamon instead)
1 teaspoon white peppercorns
1 teaspoon cardamom seeds, crush whole pods and discard the husks
1 teaspoon whole cloves
1 teaspoon freshly ground nutmeg
1/2 teaspoon ground ginger

Toast whole spices in a dry frying pan or skillet, just until fragrant. Allow to cool, add in nutmeg and ginger, and grind in a mortar and pestle or dedicated spice grinder to a fine powder. At the teahouse, Fred uses a blade coffee grinder clearly labeled "spices only." Though some spices can make an interesting addition to your morning coffee, some really don't.

Store in a glass jar with an airtight lid and try to use up within a month for best flavor.

MAJA'S HERB BOMBS

If you have some fresh herbs hanging around that are starting to lose their vivid greenness, or you just have more than you know you can get through, this is a way to preserve them. You can use any fresh herb but unless you know everyone you're cooking for is on board with cilantro/ fresh coriander, you may want to leave that one out. Parsley, basil, dill, fennel fronds (if you like the aniseed-like quality), thyme, even celery leaves are all good to go.

Pick all the leaves, removing woody or stringy stems (don't throw out your parsley stems though — you can freeze them separately to add to stocks), and add to the jar of a blender. Add enough olive oil to come about a quarter of the way up the amount of herbs you have and hit blend. You're going for a relatively smooth but not baby food-like puree. Decant your green gunge into the compartments of an ice cube try. Silicon works best for this as they are easier to unmold. Once frozen you can pop them out of the tray and store in a zip top bag or well-sealed jar in the freezer. Note: Once you make the herb oil gunge, you have to use it within a day or two or freeze it. Fresh plant matter and oil blends are subject to botulism.

To use your herb bomb, plop a frozen cube into soups or sauces, accounting for the additional oil. If you'd like to add your frozen bomb to something like scrambled eggs, I would suggest adding the herb bomb to the heated pan and letting it melt before adding the eggs. There will be almost enough oil to lubricate the pan for the eggs. You may want to add a little butter. The herbs will darken a bit and not be as pretty as freshly chopped herbs, but if you're just cooking for yourself, it's a nice way to add some flavor.

Finally, if you are into wheat grass smoothies for hangovers or for other inexplicable reasons, I can't promise an herb bomb will completely cover the field-like flavor of said grass, but the herbs and olive oil do make them a little easier to get down. Your mileage may vary.

PRESERVED LEMONS

This recipe is adapted from Paula Wolfert's *Couscous and Other Good Foods* from Morocco, though Fred does his own thing and I swear each batch is different but better than the last. (And he says he isn't a witch.) For her recipe, Wolfert recommends using Meyer lemons when they are in their brief winter season as they have a thinner, softer rind. Whatever type of lemon you use, sterilize the jar. You can easily do that by popping a freshly washed jar and its lid (unless it's plastic), on baking tray, into a 350°F (180°C) oven for 15 minutes. One other tip is to give the lemons a roll on the counter, pressing down with the palm of your hand, before quartering so they are more likely to give up their juices.

5 lemons
1/4 cup (65g) fine sea salt, more if desired
1 cinnamon stick, either Ceylon (the softer kind) or Cassia (the hard kind)
3 cloves
5 to 6 coriander seeds
3 to 4 black peppercorns
1 bay leaf
Freshly squeezed lemon juice, if necessary

Quarter the lemons from the top to within 1/2 inch of the bottom, sprinkle salt on the exposed flesh, then smoosh back together into the lemon shape.

Place 1 tablespoon salt on the bottom of a sterilized Mason jar or kilner jar. Pack in the lemons and push them down, adding more salt, and the spices between layers. Press the lemons down to release their juices and to make room for the remaining lemons. (If the juice released from the squashed fruit does not cover them, add freshly squeezed lemon juice to cover. Don't use bottled lemon juice or water. Leave some air space and seal the jar.

Let the lemons cure in a warm place, shaking the jar each day to distribute the salt and juice for 30 days. To use, rinse the lemons, as needed, under running water, removing and discarding the pulp, if desired. There is no need to refrigerate after opening, but I usually do out of habit. They'll keep up to a year.

VANILLA SUGAR

If you use a whole vanilla bean in a recipe, don't throw it out when you fish it out of the cream or syrup. Rinse it, especially if it was in a dairy product, and let it dry out on a paper towel. When dry, add it to a medium-sized jar with a tight-fitting lid and fill the jar with granulated sugar or caster sugar. Allow to sit a couple weeks in the pantry, and your sugar will take on all that lovely vanilla aroma. You can continue to add beans to the jar as you use them and top up with sugar, indefinitely.

VANILLA EXTRACT

For this you'll want to use fresh beans—at least two to start, but three is better. Place the beans in a very clean bottle, preferably with a flip top lid, but a jar will work. Now make a choice: you can fill the bottle with just vodka, or you can do half vodka and half decent but not fancy rum. I prefer the half vodka, half rum approach for the depth of flavor. Let this sit in the cupboard for at least two weeks before using. Use as you would commercial vanilla extract. You can also use the whole beans in recipes that call for them. Fish them out of whatever you made, let them dry completely, and transfer them to your vanilla sugar. Add new beans to your extract bottle once a year and top up with alcohol as needed, indefinitely.

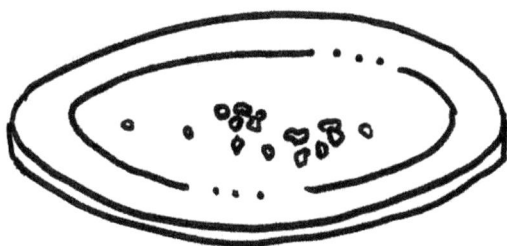

RENEGADE COOKS AT HOME

Cooking for a living doesn't absolve anyone from having to cook at home, and most professional cooks I know still enjoy making food for themselves and their near and dear. The pressure is off and you can make whatever you want and serve it however you like. You only have to please yourself and whomever you share meals with.

Professional cooks also tend to network with other people who love to cook, both at work and at home. Sharing recipes and talking food are what we do, so it isn't any wonder that everyone at Renegade Tea is surrounded by people who enjoy being in the kitchen and enjoy good food.

These are a few recipes we make for ourselves, we make for friends, and that loved ones have made for us.

TURKISH COFFEE, SLOVENIAN STYLE

Even teahouse owners need the occasional higher octane jolt of caffeine, and Slovenians are for the most part coffee drinkers. Espresso is widely available—Italy is, after all, right next door. Pour overs and French presses can be found in many homes, but this is the old school way. Every household will have its own measurements and order of operation for making coffee, but this is how I learned so that's what you're getting. Turkish coffee is made in a cezve, or what is more commonly called an ibrik in English, but a small saucepan will do in a pinch or when there is a coffee emergency.

For each person:

An espresso cup of water
1/2 teaspoon of sugar (The amount of sugar is highly debated, but it's really better with some.)
1 heaped teaspoon of very finely ground coffee (see Note)

Add all the water to the cevze or whatever you are using and bring to a boil. Remove from the heat (this is important), add all your sugar and coffee to the water, and stir thoroughly. Return to heat and don't take your eyes off it. When it just starts to bubble up, take it off the heat again and let it settle. Return it to the heat and let it start to bubble up one last time. Remove from heat and leave it to sit for a minute, allowing most of the coffee grounds to settle. Pour into coffee cups and serve black or with milk.

I rarely drink only an espresso cup's worth, so for a small coffee cup (not the industrial vat-sized ones at some U.S. coffee places, but more like a diner-sized cup), I use a level tablespoon of grounds but the same amount of sugar. Don't forget to leave that last sip in the cup, as more grounds will settle out and it can be a bit chewy at the bottom.

Note: The grind for Turkish coffee is almost like coffee powder, and most home grinders can't get coffee that fine. You can buy pre-ground coffee in small packages from Middle Eastern and Eastern European groceries. Your local supermarket or coffee shop may also have the large commercial coffee grinders that usually have a Turkish setting. And lastly, you could invest in a Turkish-grind hand mill (they are tall and skinny and often made of brass), if you'd like to use your favorite dark roast beans and don't mind a workout before you've had your morning coffee.

GREGOR'S OATMEAL PORRIDGE FOR JO

For approximately 3 servings

Unlike rolled oats, you can make a big batch of this on the weekend to have reheated for breakfast throughout the week without it going claggy and gross. Use whatever toppings make you happy, but for a special birthday breakfast, I recommend a scoop of vanilla ice cream on a warm bowl. I know ice cream on oatmeal sounds weird and possibly decadent in the extreme, but the world can be shitty and there's nothing wrong with starting the day having been kind to yourself.

2 cups (500mL) of water
1 cup (240mL) your milk of choice: cow, goat, almond, coconut, squirrel—whatevs
1 tablespoon (15g) butter, or coconut oil for vegans and nondairy folks
1 cup (160g) steel-cut oats (sometimes sold as Irish or Scottish oatmeal in the U.S.)
1/4 teaspoon salt
Gregor's mix-ins for Jo: a tablespoon of apple butter (see Pantry), a dash of cinnamon, and a splash of cold milk

In a large saucepan with a lid, bring the milk and water to a simmer over medium heat. Melt in the butter or coconut oil. While that's heating, toast the oats in a dry sauté pan over medium-high heat until they have darkened in color and smell toasty—about two minutes. It's tempting to skip this step. If you do, your oatmeal will taste fine, but toasting the oats first brings breakfast up several notches.

Add your toasty oats to the simmering liquid and add the salt. You may have to play with the temperature to get a bare simmer. Cover and let cook about 20 minutes, stirring occasionally while you make coffee or whatever, until the oats are thickened. Take a quick taste to see if the oats are to your liking. I like mine done but with a bit of bounce still. You may need to cook them up to an additional 10 minutes, adding a little water if the porridge gets too thick so it doesn't scorch.

Remove from the heat, stir in the apple butter and cinnamon, and serve in your favorite bowl with your favorite spoon with a splash of cold milk on top.

JO'S LEMON DAL

I'm not much of a believer in the authentic versus inauthentic food debates. Classic recipes all over the world have regional variants, and every cook makes a dish their own. A good takeaway curry in London is as authentic a curry as one made in a Kerala home kitchen. I had this, or a version of it, in a Brick Lane curry shop the first time I visited London with Rok and Faron. In trying to recreate its wonderful sourness, I hit upon using lemon. The original, I suspect, is made with amchur, a tangy green mango powder that isn't always easy to get your hands on. (Though it's easier now that you can order anything you could possibly want online.) It looks a little nicer if the dal holds its shape, but I like mine a little mushier, the texture of next day leftovers. It's my ultimate comfort food and has the power to evoke the memory of a long dead friend I shared a plate of this with.

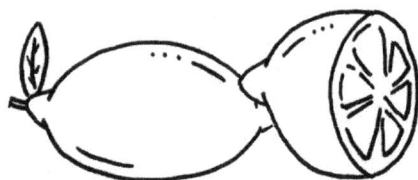

1 tablespoon ghee or butter

3 cloves garlic, minced

1 small onion, chopped

*2 cups (450g) matar dal, also called chana dal (Yellow split peas are
a good substitute.)*

4 cups (950mL) of water

1/2 inch piece of ginger, peeled

1 teaspoon cumin

1/4 teaspoon cayenne

1 teaspoon ground turmeric

1 teaspoon sea salt

2 lemons

1/2 teaspoon white pepper

1 teaspoon garam masala

Optional topping:

3 tablespoons butter

1 teaspoon whole cumin

1 clove garlic

Pinch red pepper flakes

Fresh cilantro, chopped

Plain yogurt, stirred until smooth

In a large saucepan, melt ghee or butter and sauté garlic and onion
until the onion is translucent.

While the onion and garlic are doing their thing, sort the dal or peas
and pick out any stones or odd looking bits. Give them a rinse and add
to the onions with the ginger, cumin, cayenne, turmeric, and salt. Stir
this around to coat everything in the oil and toast the spices a bit. Add
water, bring to a boil, then reduce heat to simmer 20 to 40 minutes or
until soft enough to smoosh a legume or two against the side of the

pan and some are starting to break down. This may take longer than 40 minutes, depending on the age of said legumes.

Once the dal is to your liking, remove from heat. Squeeze in the juice of two lemons and add the white pepper and garam masala. Taste for seasoning. If it isn't sour or lemony enough, you can add more lemon juice or a little zest from one of the lemons.

For an extra flourish, heat three tablespoons of butter in a small frying pan. When it's bubbling, add a teaspoon of whole cumin seed and a clove or two of garlic sliced very thinly. Stir that around until the garlic is just lightly browned and smells toasty. Remove from heat and add a pinch of red pepper flakes, if you're up for more spice. Do not add the chili flakes to the hot butter while it's on the heat unless you want to clear your house with the culinary equivalent of tear gas. Drizzle a spoonful over each portion before serving.

Top each bowl with a little yogurt, strew over some chopped cilantro (haters can substitute flat-leaf parsley), and serve with basmati rice, an Indian pickle or chutney, and some warm naan.

APPLE CHAAT

Chaat masala is a snack spice mix that is usually applied to carbs. It can, however, be applied to anything snacky—so fruit and veg are fair game, as are fries or chips. Apples are my go-to, but it's great on pineapple, mango, cantaloupe, jicama, pears—you are only limited by your imagination and availability. Easy Mode is an adaptation of the more traditional recipe that tries to capture the flavors of the traditional mix with spices found at your average, well-stocked supermarket. The Advanced Mode recipe shared here is adapted from a Serious Eats one by Sohla El-Waylly—she is a cooking genius you need to know—and will require treasure hunting excursions to local international food markets or an online order.

Chaat masala - Easy Mode:

2 1/2 tablespoons cumin seeds
1 tablespoon coriander seeds
1 1/2 tablespoon fennel seeds
1 1/2 teaspoons caraway seeds
1 tablespoon dried mint
1 teaspoon large flake, kosher salt
1 teaspoon whole black peppercorns
5 teaspoons ancho chili powder (can sub cayenne but use way less, start with 1/2 teaspoon and taste, as cayenne is much hotter than ancho)
1 teaspoon ground ginger
1 to 2 teaspoons apple cider vinegar, or a squeeze of fresh lime juice

Chaat masala - Advanced Mode:

2 1/2 tablespoons cumin seeds
1 tablespoon coriander seeds
1 1/2 tablespoon fennel seeds
1 1/2 teaspoons ajwain seeds
1 tablespoon dried mint
1 tablespoon kala namak powder (also known as black salt or
Himalayan black salt), see Note
1 teaspoon large flake, kosher salt
3 tablespoons amchur (green mango powder)
4 1/2 teaspoons tamarind powder
1 teaspoon whole black peppercorns
5 teaspoons Kashmiri red chili powder
1 teaspoon ground ginger
Tart eating apples—about half a large apple per person, cored and
sliced thinly.

For either version, toast the seeds one spice at a time in a dry sauté pan just until each is warm and fragrant. Set them aside together in a bowl to cool.

Add the seeds and all the remaining ingredients to a spice grinder. A blade coffee grinder is good for this, but dedicate one to grinding spices. You can also use a mortar and pestle if you're feeling witchy and or chef-y or don't have a spice mill or coffee grinder. Grind to a fine powder. You may have to do this in batches, depending on the capacity of your spice grinding apparatus.

This makes around a cup, so you can make a batch to keep around for when the mood strikes you. It will stay fresh in an airtight jar for up to a month.

Fan out thinly sliced apples on a plate or platter. If you are using the easy spice mix, sprinkle the apples with the cider vinegar or lime juice, then hit the apples with a dusting of the spice mixture. Serve to hungry guests (or a waiting shade) before dinner or as a snack.

Note: Kala namak brings a slightly sulfurous and funky note with a definite umami flavor to the spice party. If you can't find it, you can leave it out and your Advanced Mode mix will still taste lovely. If you can track it down, though, it's worth the effort. It's also a great addition to vegetarian curries and can be used in the place of fish sauce in vegan recipes for that funky note.

GRANDMA ROSE'S CLOVERLEAF ROLLS

These taste of home and Sunday dinners at my grandmother's house. They are an easy recipe to tackle, even if you're bread phobic. I warn you, though, once these enter your baking lexicon, they work their way into heavy rotation. These are best warm, served with honey butter, "for special," as Grandma Rose would say.

1 package (1/4 ounce or 7g) active, dry yeast
2 tablespoons granulated sugar
1/2 cup (120mL) whole milk, warmed 105°-110°F (40°-43°C)
2 cups (255g) all-purpose flour
1 teaspoon kosher salt
1 large egg, beaten
6 tablespoons (85g) unsalted butter, softened, plus more to butter pan and some melted to brush the tops

In a small bowl or measuring cup, combine yeast, warmed milk, and a teaspoon of the sugar. Set this aside to get foamy, about 5 minutes.

While the yeast is doing its thing, combine remaining sugar, flour, and salt in the bowl of a stand mixer set up with the dough hook. With the mixer on low, pour in the yeast mixture and then the egg. Mix until things are well-combined and a smooth dough is formed, increasing speed to medium-low. This may take 5 to 10 minutes, and you may need to stop the mixer and scrape down the sides of the bowl a couple of times.

Once the dough is formed, return mixer to low speed and add the softened butter. The dough will slide around around a bit, but eventually all the butter will be incorporated into the dough. Continue kneading the dough until it's shiny and elastic, gradually increasing the speed again to medium.

Scrape the dough off the hook and into a ball in the center of the bowl. Cover with a plate or plastic wrap and set it aside in a warm place to rise until doubled in size. This will take one to two hours, depending on how hot it is in your kitchen.

While the dough is rising, generously butter the cups of a standard 12-cup muffin pan.

When the dough has doubled, tip it out onto a clean work surface—you shouldn't need any flour, but if it is sticking a little, very lightly dust the board and your hands. Divide the dough into 12 equal pieces. You can use a scale if you are going for gold-star uniformity, or you can just eyeball it. Work with one piece at a time, leaving the others covered with a clean tea towel. Divide each portion of the dough into three equal pieces and roll each into a ball. (This means you should, all told, make 36 balls of dough.) Nestle the three pieces together in one layer in a muffin cup. Repeat with the remaining portions.

Cover the muffin pan lightly with an oiled piece of plastic wrap or a thin tea towel lightly dusted with flour. The second rise will take 45 minutes to an hour, again depending on how warm it is where the dough is hanging out.

Toward the end of the rise, preheat your oven to 375°F (190°C). Very gently brush the top of each roll with melted butter and bake until puffed and golden brown, 10–12 minutes.

Brush with yet more melted butter and serve Grandma Rose-style in a basket lined with a checked tea towel. If you are serving a crowd, it's best to double the batch as a few always disappear before the basket hits the dinner table.

FUNERAL CAKE

In the American South, funerals mean food. This can be a meal after the service itself, held at a church or at the home of the family who has suffered a loss. More and more this seems to happen at a local restaurant to ease the burden on the family of hosting and on the attendees of bringing a dish. Even if there isn't a dinner, neighbors, friends, and family bring food to the bereaved. It is both a way of showing kindness toward the grieving and a concrete way of reminding us that we are still alive and must tend to the needs of the living body. This traditional pound cake, as made by my Aunt Jackie's best friend, Martha, incorporates rosemary for remembrance, and its piney scent offers a pleasant culinary surprise. Make with intention and wait until it has cooled completely to package for gifting.

1/2 pound (1 cup, 225g) butter, softened
1/2 pound (225g) granulated sugar (approximately 1 cup plus 2 tablespoons)
1/2 pound (225g) eggs (4 large eggs plus one egg yolk)
2 teaspoons grated lemon zest
1 tablespoon very finely chopped fresh rosemary
1 teaspoon vanilla extract
1/2 pound (225g) all-purpose flour (approximately 1 1/2 cups plus 1 tablespoon)
1/2 teaspoon salt

Glaze:

3/4 cups (75g) confectioner's (icing or powdered) sugar, sifted
1/2 teaspoon grated lemon zest
1 tablespoon lemon juice

one sprig of fresh rosemary, for decorating

Preheat oven to 350°F (180°C), Grease and flour one standard loaf pan (8.5 inches x 4.5 inches or 23x13cm).

In a large bowl, cream butter and sugar until light and fluffy. Incorporate one egg at a time, beating well after each addition. Beat in the lemon zest, rosemary, and vanilla extract. In a separate bowl, whisk together the flour and salt. Fold the flour into the butter, sugar, and egg mixture just until incorporated.

Scrape the mixture into the prepared loaf pan and bake 45-50 minutes, or until a toothpick tests clean when inserted into the thickest part of the cake. Cool the baked cake on a rack for 10 minutes before removing from the pan and allowing to cool completely.

When the cake is cooled, combine the confectioner's sugar and zest and add enough of the lemon juice to make a spoonable but not runny icing. Drizzle this over the cooled cake and position the rosemary sprig down the center of the loaf before the glaze dries to help it stick the top. The unglazed cake can be wrapped and frozen and glazed after thawing unwrapped at room temperature. The flavor of the cake develops overnight, so consider making it a day ahead of when you plan to serve it, and don't feel like you have to save the recipe for a sad occasion. You can make this anytime.

The recipe can be doubled using 9 whole large eggs and 1 1/2 tablespoons rosemary, but don't double the salt. Bake in a standard 12-cup (2.8L) Bundt pan for about the same total baking time.

SHAKSHOUKA FOR MINNIE

Serves 4

Shakshouka is served in Algeria for breakfast, but also as a dish to break the fast at iftar during Ramadan. Fred made this version to prove to Minnie that a full-English brown and beige breakfast was not the be-all end-all of breakfasts. You can make this as fiery as you like by adjusting the amount of harissa. However spicy you make it, it may become your new favorite breakfast.

1/4 cup (60mL) extra virgin olive oil
1 large yellow onion, diced
4 large garlic cloves, peeled and minced
1 pound (500g) merguez sausage, chopped or crumbled (can substitute chorizo or omit for vegetarian version)
1 tablespoon ras al hanout (see Pantry)
1 teaspoon smoked paprika
1 teaspoon kosher salt
1 tablespoon harissa (see Pantry)
2, 14.5-ounce cans (411g) fire roasted, crushed tomatoes (can also use diced, if you prefer)
4 to 8 eggs, depending on how many eggs people want and how many you can fit in your pan
1/2 cup (large handful) cilantro, chopped (haters can sub flat-leafed parsley)
4 tablespoons (2 ounces/60g) goat cheese, crumbled

Heat olive oil in a large skillet or sauteuse with a lid, add onion, and sauté until golden brown. (Avoid using a cast-iron for this because of the acidity of the tomatoes.) Add garlic and cook an additional minute, then add sausage (if using) and cook until sausage is almost cooked through. If the sausage has released too much fat into the pan, you can spoon it off, leaving about a tablespoon.

Add the ras al hanout, smoked paprika, and salt to the pan, allowing the spices to toast (or, more accurately, fry) until their aromas are released. Add harissa and tomatoes and cook until the mixture begins to thicken, anywhere from 15 to 30 minutes. Taste for seasoning and add salt if needed.

Make a few wells in the mixture to accommodate the number of eggs you are cooking, and crack an egg into each depression. Put the lid on, slightly askew so steam can still escape, and cook until the whites are set and the yolks are done to your preference. Thickly runny for me, please, at about 4 minutes. For harder cooked yolks, steam closer to 8 minutes.

To serve, use a large spoon to gently lift out eggs onto plates or into shallow bowls, divide remaining sauce among the servings. Scatter over cilantro (or parsley) and goat cheese. Serve hot with a chunk of fresh baguette and some good, strong coffee.

SPELLS & STUFF

Witchcraft is a tool. Like any tool you fashion yourself, you will personalize it and cobble it together from examples you've seen. You may also research the history of that tool or what others have to say about it. You will tweak it over time so it better fits your hand or your purpose. Chances are you may have to repair it along the way. I'm not here to tell you how to make a wooden spoon, but I'll show you the one I made and happily explain how I got there. Like the recipes that came before this section of the book, these are suggested instructions to get you to a final result. There are certainly other ways to get things done, and, just like the recipes, I hope you'll use these as a jumping off point rather than a prescription.

A BLACK CANDLE FOR MORANA

Black candles get a bad rap. They tend to be associated with "black magic" and are often used by the media and anti-witchcraft factions as shorthand for baby eating and cat skinning in the woods. The magic is in the witch, not the object, necessarily, and magic itself is neither black nor white. A witch can hex or heal for good or evil.

Objects can have a mind of their own, like hand-me-down wands. But candles are generally just candles, and black is a color of protection. When doing any spells or other witchy things, like making dinner, it doesn't hurt to light a candle to ask your deity of choice for a little protection in your working. In our local tradition we honor Morana, Queen of the Witches.

As not all witches work with deities, the candle can also be used to ask for protection from or to honor your ancestors in your work, or it can simply be a point of focus for your attention to the task at hand.

When you've finished your work, extinguish the candle by snuffing it or by clapping close to the flame. Those with asbestos hands can also pinch out the flame. Many witches avoid blowing out candles—except those on birthday cakes?—for various reasons. Others don't care and happily blow out every and all candles. You do you.

Oh, and the candle doesn't necessarily have to be black. Witches make do.

WITCH'S BLACK SALT

Black salt is the invention of modern witches, so you can do as you choose. Many witches make black salt by mixing charcoal and the ashes of ritual or sacred fires with sea or mined salt. Working in kitchens and being somewhat obsessed with all the different varieties of salt, I also like to use culinary black salts, such as those from Hawaii and Cyprus. I also like to use the sulfurous black Himalayan salt that is used in the vegetarian cuisines where it is mined and produced. This black salt is made by kiln-firing pink Himalayan salt. It is a gray color in larger crystal form and a smoky pink color when ground fine. It also smells of sulfur, giving it that extra-witchy, fire and brimstone vibe.

Whatever salt you choose to use in ritual, store it airtight and keep it dry, dispose of it properly after use, and don't store witch's black salt with your culinary black salts or where it could be confused for culinary salt. Witch's black salt should never be consumed.

HERBS FOR YOUR SCRYING BOWL

A scrying bowl is a low flat bowl made of black-fired or black glazed pottery, often used filled with rainwater or water the moon has shined on to gaze into the future or look for answers to questions we carry in our own consciousness. In the magic traditions of our local witches, it is also used as a stand-in for a cauldron in spells used to summon spirits of the dead, break hexes, and other magical workings and potion creations that don't require heat.

The best herbs for use in magic are the ones you have access to, including those in your spice rack and the unnoticed ones in your lawn or nearby surroundings. There are many, many books that can help you learn about the magical and medicinal uses of herbs. Those can be incredibly helpful, but also consider books that are for identifying trees and plants in your local area and books written by foragers and wildcrafters.

For magical purposes you can ask the plant what it does. Always ask the plant for permission before harvesting, and leave plenty to sustain the plant and the local fauna that may depend on it. Ask for permission from an actual human when harvesting on private land, and know the local law for harvesting on public land. You can grow many culinary and magical herbs, even in pots on a sunny windowsill. There is no witch shame in buying dried or fresh herbs from farmers or herb purveyors, but always establish if the herbs are for culinary use if you plan to consume them. Never consume any wild-harvested herbs if you aren't 100 percent certain on the identification. Many safe wild herbs have poisonous cousins or near look-alikes. To paraphrase the aphorism about mushroom hunters: there are old witches and bold witches, but there are no old, bold witches who ate random plants for shits and giggles.

For a specific recipe of herbs to sprinkle in your scrying bowl when attempting to gaze into the future, Ivanka favors a little bit of mugwort and rosemary with a star anise pod thrown in for protection.

LAYING PROTECTIVE SALT

Witches—Voices of the Dead, especially—deserve some peace in their own homes. This ritual allows a witch to set the parameters for what is allowed in. According to Aunt Jackie, all you need is salt. Choose a type of salt that is meaningful for you—sea salt from a certain place, black salt, witch's black salt, whatever.

Place the salt in in a bowl and hold it in your hands. Visualize the envelope of your home as a bubble, the filmy edge of which is impenetrable to shades and spirits. You can imagine them being repelled by the bubble or bouncing off the membrane if they try to get through. The imagery should be something that works for you.

Now imagine the shades or spirits you don't mind sharing your space with. Visualize them finding a door in your bubble and walking through, closing the door behind them.

Take your bowl and sprinkle salt at the threshold of exterior doors and on every windowsill. If you have enough salt and there is a way to lay a line of salt at each door so that it won't be disturbed, that is best but a sprinkling will do.

Very cautious witches also sprinkle some salt at ventilation points and on fireplaces—any entrance to your home, maybe even sinks, tubs, and toilets. It's best to renew this ward yearly.

A note from Vesna: If you live with pets or small children who might find your salt tempting, dissolve your salt into warm water, wash all the thresholds, sills, and openings with the water, and allow them to air dry.

WITCH BELLS

Witch bells are a simple addition to your salt warding, but they can also be used by themselves.

For this charm, you will need:

At least two or three bells (Brass or silver are nice, but any type will work.)
A length of cord or ribbon
Optional trinkets or beads for additional protection

Thread your bells onto the cord or ribbon and tie them near the center of the length. Larger bells can be tied together, or you can tie them spaced out in a way that allows them to chime against each other when the cord is swung (as it will be on a door). Add any additional trinkets for protection, such as stone or glass beads, coins, or figurative charms. Then tie the ends together leaving a large enough loop to go over the doorknob or handle.

Hang your bells on the inside handle of your door. Ring the bells with a brush of your hand and visualize that sound as repellent to anyone who would endeavor to do your home, your business, or you and your loved ones any harm. If the bells are for your business, take note if a patron is annoyed by the bells. You may find them a troublesome customer. For your home, it is advisable to make a charm for each exterior door. You can also make one for your bedroom door, especially if you live with other people or you sleep with your door closed.

Don't forget to pack them with you if you move. To recharge the ward, brush your hand over them anytime you think to do so—especially after someone leaves who has brought any negative energy into your home or after a visitor leaves who you would prefer not visit again.

WITCH BOTTLES

Witch bottles are an old form of magic that goes back to at least 17th century England and were most likely brought to what is now North America by English colonizers and settlers. Early witch bottles were often made by filling clay vessels with objects and liquids believed to protect a dwelling from the negative influence of witches. Multiples of things like rice or sand were included so that a demon would be forced to count every grain before entering. These jugs were also filled with needles, nails, and sometimes urine to make them more potent.

Modern witches make witch jars to ward off malevolent or bothersome spirits and negative influences of the mundane and supernatural varieties. Bottles or jars are filled with herbs, rice, salt, needles, nails, lengths of string or wire, thumbtacks, pins, and protective herbs and are topped off with wine or water or left dry. You can still pee in it, of course, if that's your thing. The magic is in the intent of the witch, so fill yours how you choose and take Aunt Jackie's recipe as a starting point.

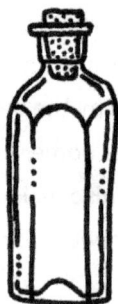

AUNT JACKIE'S WITCH JAR FOR PROTECTION FROM BOTHERSOME SHADES

Small glass jar or bottle with a tight-fitting lid or stopper
Thumbtacks, nails, or needles
Pieces of string
White rice
Salt
Protective herbs: rosemary, bay leaves, basil, hot pepper, black pepper, garlic
White wine or vinegar

Place your sharp objects in the jar. A couple will do; you don't have to fill it. Add your bits of string or lengths of wire. Mix your rice, salt, and whatever herbs you are using together in a bowl and stir in your intention to protect your home from bothersome shades and unwanted influences. They are not welcome in your space. Fill the jar with the mixture, top up with white wine or vinegar, and seal the jar.

You can mark the lid or stopper with a protective symbol like a watchful eye or a five-pointed star.

Bury the jar under the threshold of or next to the front door. If you move, dig up the jar and take it with you to your next house. If the jar can't be recovered, on the day you move, stand as close to it as you can get and thank it for protecting you and your home. Release the energy to serve whoever lives there next or to disperse as it wishes.

Note for apartment dwellers or if you are unable to bury the jar outside: Find a hidden location near your front door or in the easternmost part of your apartment or home, and remember to take it with you when you leave.

SORTILEGE

Sortilege is simply the casting of lots. What those lots are can vary widely culture to culture, but they can include sticks, stones, bones, beans, coins, or things like Nordic runes, the Irish ogham, Chinese mahjong tiles or the I Ching. Modern oracle decks are also a type of sortilege. All of these are, with the exception of the oracle cards that are usually dealt like tarot, "thrown" onto a surface or cloth, then interpreted by the reader. Sets and books for interpretation for these set systems are widely available.

But there is another type of sortilege, often just called sortilege, in which the lots consist of many of the items mentioned above plus small trinkets or figurines, keys, shells, and other found objects. The power of this collection approach is that the reader has assembled all of the items themselves, so the objects have meaning to the reader more so than the traditional meanings associated with them. A key may represent an open door, escape, or be emblematic of a figure or deity such as Hecate, known by one of her many names as the Keeper of the Keys. It could also simply represent home, especially if the key is one from the reader's current or previous house or apartment.

Some readers also mark the cloth the collection of lots is thrown onto. Some use a circle, and the items that fall inside the circle represent internal forces and those outside represent external ones. The cloth can also be divided into thirds or quadrants. The sections could mean past, present, future or represent the four elements or cardinal directions. Every reader has their own method of interpretation.

If you wish to assemble your own sortilege collection, you can begin with a bag to hold your items and add to it over time. Common items are, keys, beans, the dried pods of plants, small porcelain figurines, wishbones and other small animal bones, stones or crystals, dice, coins—especially foreign ones or tokens—pieces of broken china or pottery, dollhouse miniatures, jewelry such as a single earring or a ring, a paper clip or safety pin, shells, sharks' teeth, beach glass, a tiny mirror, a baby tooth, small toys, and so on.

Some natural items may break down over time and need to be replaced. Very fragile items are not recommended, as the items are usually stored together in the bag and thrown or dumped out on a surface or cloth for a reading. The collection can be added to or edited over time as the reader's relationship with the items changes. There's no wrong way to to do this, but the reader may find how they cast or throw and interpret changes over time as their confidence and familiarity with their assortment grows.

MAKING A PENDULUM WITH WHAT YOU HAVE

At many occult stores, witch markets, or online retailers, you can find pendulums from the simple to the sublime at any price point you can imagine. But you can also make a pendulum with many common items at hand. A ring and a necklace chain make a simple and efficient pendulum. Many "old wives" have tried to predict the sex of unborn babies with the mother's wedding ring on a chain. Any object with enough heft to swing on a chain, cord, or string can be a pendulum, but its having some significance or meaning to you may help you connect to it.

To calibrate your pendulum, before each use, hold the chain or string with the weight about 2 inches (4cm) above your palm. Ask a simple yes or no question, such as, "Is my name [whatever your name is]?" The direction your pendulum swings is yes, the opposite is no. Usually those motions are back and forth, perpendicular and parallel to the user, but your pendulum may calibrate to yes and no being clockwise and anti-clockwise in a circle.

Other movements of the pendulum can be determined different ways by different users, such as swinging in a circle means "maybe" or "unclear" when the yes and no have been established as back and forth motions. An unmoving pendulum is often interpreted as "no answer now" or "don't ask that question."

Whatever you use and however it is calibrated, pendulums are best for yes or no questions or questions with a choice of two answers. They can also be used with other forms of divination for clarification and are a pleasant way to interact with fellow witches over tea.

HEX BREAKING SPELL

According to the book passed down from Breda to her son Goran and now to Ivanka, this spell is good for breaking hexes and also for releasing the enchantment from needy or troublesome magical objects. As Goran learned from the burnt circle on his ceiling, if you are working with a particularly strong or old magic object, it's best to perform this outdoors. You never quite know exactly how these types of spells will go.

Spell components

Collected rainwater
A small piece of angelica root
2 leaves of bay laurel
A smashed clove of garlic
3 mistletoe berries (handle with caution: poisonous)
A sprig of fresh rosemary
A small bunch of dried or fresh pine needles
A pinch each of:
    aniseed
    dried cyclamen petals
    dried heliotrope petals
    dried black hellebore petals
    dried stinging nettle leaves
    dried rue leaves
    dried vervain
Pine or fir incense (cone, stick, or loose is fine)
A small piece of black tourmaline
A black beeswax candle
A shallow black pottery bowl
Black salt

Prepare your working space. This will be unique to each practitioner. In Breda's book of magical recipes, she instructed that a circle of black salt be laid down to prevent whatever is inside the magical object from escaping. She also instructs the practitioner to light a black candle to honor Morana, Queen of the Witches, and ask for her protection in your working.

Once your space is prepared, fill your bowl with rainwater and add all the herbs and place the tourmaline in the bottom of the bowl. You can use a very small piece of the stone. Light your incense.

Hold the magical item in your hand and thank it for the work you have done together. Recite these words:

This [name of item] no longer serves me. I release the magic bound within that it may return to the source of all magic.*

Place the object in the bowl and maybe step back. Depending on the power contained within the object, nothing may happen or the whole thing could blow up. This is why some kind of containment is important.

To break a hex, use the spell bundle or object used to hex you, if you can find it, or create a tag lock to the person you believe hexed you by writing their name on a piece of paper.

Hold the object or tag lock above the bowl and recite these words:

I undo the intent of this hex and render it harmless against me and those I protect. I release the magic in this working to dissipate into the wind and the water and the earth.

Then drop the object or tag lock into the bowl as above.

If you are the hexing type, you can reflect the energy of the hex back onto the person who cast it by using these words instead:

I undo the intent of this hex and render it harmless against me and those I protect. May the intent of this magic be reflected on the one who would do me and mine harm.

When you are finished, thank Morana for her presence and extinguish the candle. Depending on your affinity to the elements, you can dispose of spell materials and what remains of the object by burning, burying, or disposing in running water.

Notes from Ivanka:

*You can say any of these phrases in Latin, if that's your thing, but the magic of language and the language of magic is far older than the Romans. Words in the language or languages you speak carry just as much power.

If I've learned anything about magic, it's that all these elaborate spells and gathering of often obscure herbs aren't strictly necessary. The elements themselves are enough to dispel unwanted or no longer needed magic; burn it, bury it, or return it to running water—with the caveat that you shouldn't add anything harmful to the ecosystem, and any plastics should be disposed of according to local regulations. Also, don't bury parts of non-native or invasive species of plants. Finally, the candle for your deity of choice isn't a bad idea, but know that nature itself is a source of magic.

READING TEA LEAVES

Reading tea leaves is a form of divination or scrying called tasseomancy. The difference between peering into a dark bowl of water or the smoke of a fire and looking at tea leaves is that you definitely have something to look at in the clumps of spent leaves, and you have the cup itself to give you a sense of time in the reading.

To read the leaves, make your querent a cup of tea with loose-leaf tea. Instead of straining the tea leaves out of the pot, let the leaves remain in the tea and in the cup. For this reason, a tea that doesn't mind a longer steeping can be a good idea. Either that or drink it relatively quickly so you don't have to drink stewed tea. While the querent is drinking their tea, ask them to think of what questions they have or why they want someone to take a glance into their future.

When all but the last sip of the tea has been drunk, swirl the cup—three times is traditional. Cover the cup with an upside-down saucer and turn the cup and saucer over, allowing the remaining liquid to drain onto the saucer. You should be left with damp leaves stuck to the sides and bottom of an otherwise empty cup.

Hold the cup in your hand with the handle, which represents the querent, pointed toward you, the reader. Leaves closer to the handle represent things close to the person you are reading for, such as internal forces and things in the querent's immediate surroundings. Things farther from the handle represent more external forces. For the timing of events, the rim represents the querent's present. What you see further from the rim indicates it is further away in time, the bottom of the cup being the distant future. It could also be the distant past if the person you're reading for has asked a question that involves interpreting things from their past.

But what do the leaves themselves mean? There are a couple of schools of thought here. Reading tea leaves can be a bit like sortilege: the meanings of the shapes the reader sees will depend on the associations that reader has with those shapes. So what is to be seen? How do you see it?

Soften your gaze into the cup and see if the arrangement of any of the leaves suggest a shape to you. It's a bit like looking at clouds imagining flying dragons and sword-fighting cats. Our brains are wired to look for patterns, and especially faces, in the chaos. That part isn't magic. How you interpret what you see is where the magic lies.

There are traditional meanings for different shapes—anchors for travel, a castle for unexpected wealth, a cow for prosperity, snakes for a bad omen. There are tons of books and websites dedicated to sorting out what each symbol means, and there is a kind of collected energy in those traditional meanings. You don't have to memorize them or keep a cheat sheet nearby.

Instead think about what an anchor means to you. For me, it is more about being weighed down or tied to a place or an idea. A snake represents knowledge, like the twin snakes on the Rod of Asclepius used to represent healing. A castle means dreams. Is it in the air or is it grounded in reality?

If you run across something you don't know how to interpret, ask the querent. They are an equal participant in this adventure. "Does a fishhook mean anything to you?" Once you know that symbol reminds them of fishing with their grandmother when they were a child, you can look at the context around it and where it is in the cup to derive further meaning.

Remember that whatever you see in that cup is a glimpse of a possible future or a glance at the rich personal history of your querent seen through the lens of the present moment. The future is not written in stone, and we reinterpret our own past through new lived experience every time we remember. Whatever the leaves tell you is predicated on that time and place, and our individual choices can swirl the cup for a different outcome or perspective.

INDEX

C

R

S

V

W

Y

YOUR NOTES

YOUR NOTES

YOUR NOTES